Microsoft® Office 2010

Transition from Office 2003

Microsoft® Office 2010: Transition from Office 2003

Part Number: 084574
Course Edition: 1.1

NOTICES

HELP US IMPROVE OUR COURSEWARE

Microsoft® Office 2010: Transition from Office 2003

Lesson 1: Getting Started with Microsoft Office 2010

A. Customize the User Interface 2

B. Work with Ribbon Tabs 14

C. Save Files in Different Formats............................... 21

D. Print Files 27

Lesson 2: Modifying Documents Using Microsoft Word 2010

A. Navigate and Find Information 34

B. Apply Text Styles 39

C. Add SmartArt Graphics...................................... 49

D. Insert Screenshots in a Document 56

E. Compare Reviewed Documents 61

Lesson 3: Working with Spreadsheets Using Microsoft Excel 2010

A. Work with Tables 68

B. Apply a Formula 72

C. Apply Enhanced Conditional Formatting 79

D. Create Charts 83

E. Create Sparklines.. 90

F. Work with PivotTables and PivotCharts 93

Lesson 4: Creating Dynamic Presentations Using Microsoft PowerPoint 2010

A. Apply Themes 104

B. Apply Picture Effects....................................... 110

C. Apply Animation and Transition Effects 116

D. Add Videos 122

E. Divide a Presentation into Sections 127

Lesson 5: Working with Databases Using Microsoft Access 2010

A. Work with Tables 134

B. Work with Queries and Macros............................... 143

C. Create Forms 151

D. Create Reports... 158

E. Work with External Data 166

F. Design a Database for the Web 172

Lesson 6: Managing Information at Work with Microsoft Outlook 2010

A. Manage Email Messages..................................... 182

B. Locate Information Quickly 191

C. Share Calendar Information 196

D. Share Contact Information 207

E. Add RSS Feeds... 217

Lesson 7: Sharing Microsoft Office 2010 Files

A. Protect Files 222

B. Share Files 228

Lesson Labs... 237

Glossary 245

Index 249

About This Course

Having worked with the applications in *Microsoft® Office 2003*, you must also get to know the features present in the latest release of the application. *Microsoft® Office 2010: Transition from Office 2003* focuses on the enhanced features for improving the management, organization, presentation, and distribution of data. In this course, you will work with the new features in Office 2010.

When projects and deadlines are piling up, it is necessary to streamline your tasks and maximize productivity. *Microsoft® Office 2010* helps you achieve this with its new user-friendly interface, along with a host of new and enhanced results-oriented features. Even if you will be using the Office 2010 application only to create and format documents, it is important to have a working knowledge of the interface changes and the enhanced capabilities. This will help when you want to create better documents by using features that are not only enhanced, but are also simple and non-time consuming.

Course Description

Target Student

Users with prior experience of previous versions of the Microsoft Office suite, who are looking to transition to 2010 and want to know what the new features of Office 2010 are.

Course Prerequisites

To be successful in this course, you should be familiar with prior versions of the Microsoft Office suite of products (Word, Excel, PowerPoint, Access, and Outlook). To ensure your success, we recommend you first take one of Element K's Level 1 courses, such as either of the following, or have equivalent skills and knowledge:

- *Microsoft® Office Word® 2003: Level 1*
- *Microsoft® Office Excel® 2003 Level 1*
- *Microsoft® Office PowerPoint® 2003 Level 1*
- *Microsoft® Office Access® 2003 Level 1*
- *Microsoft® Office Outlook® 2003 Level 1*

Course Objectives

In this course, you will work with the new and updated features of Microsoft Office 2010.

You will:

- Identify the new and enhanced features that are common to all applications in the Microsoft Office suite.
- Modify documents using Microsoft Word 2010.
- Present worksheet data using Microsoft Excel 2010.
- Create dynamic presentations using Microsoft PowerPoint 2010
- Work with databases using Microsoft Access 2010.
- Manage tasks using the new features in Microsoft Outlook 2010.
- Share files using Microsoft Office 2010.

How to Use This Book

As a Learning Guide

This book is divided into lessons and topics, covering a subject or a set of related subjects. In most cases, lessons are arranged in order of increasing proficiency.

The results-oriented topics include relevant and supporting information you need to master the content. Each topic has various types of activities designed to enable you to practice the guidelines and procedures as well as to solidify your understanding of the informational material presented in the course.

At the back of the book, you will find a glossary of the definitions of the terms and concepts used throughout the course. You will also find an index to assist in locating information within the instructional components of the book.

In the Classroom

This book is intended to enhance and support the in-class experience. Procedures and guidelines are presented in a concise fashion along with activities and discussions. Information is provided for reference and reflection in such a way as to facilitate understanding and practice.

Each lesson may also include a Lesson Lab or various types of simulated activities. You will find the files for the simulated activities along with the other course files on the enclosed CD-ROM. If your course manual did not come with a CD-ROM, please go to **http://elementkcourseware.com** to download the files. If included, these interactive activities enable you to practice your skills in an immersive business environment, or to use hardware and software resources not available in the classroom. The course files that are available on the CD-ROM or by download may also contain sample files, support files, and additional reference materials for use both during and after the course.

As a Teaching Guide

Effective presentation of the information and skills contained in this book requires adequate preparation. As such, as an instructor, you should familiarize yourself with the content of the entire course, including its organization and approaches. You should review each of the student activities and exercises so you can facilitate them in the classroom.

Throughout the book, you may see Instructor Notes that provide suggestions, answers to problems, and supplemental information for you, the instructor. You may also see references to "Additional Instructor Notes" that contain expanded instructional information; these notes appear in a separate section at the back of the book. PowerPoint slides may be provided on the included course files, which are available on the enclosed CD-ROM or by download from http://elementkcourseware.com. The slides are also referred to in the text. If you plan to use the slides, it is recommended to display them during the corresponding content as indicated in the instructor notes in the margin.

The course files may also include assessments for the course, which can be administered diagnostically before the class, or as a review after the course is completed. These exam-type questions can be used to gauge the students' understanding and assimilation of course content.

As a Review Tool

Any method of instruction is only as effective as the time and effort you, the student, are willing to invest in it. In addition, some of the information that you learn in class may not be important to you immediately, but it may become important later. For this reason, we encourage you to spend some time reviewing the content of the course after your time in the classroom.

As a Reference

The organization and layout of this book make it an easy-to-use resource for future reference. Taking advantage of the glossary, index, and table of contents, you can use this book as a first source of definitions, background information, and summaries.

Course Icons

Icon	Description
	A **Caution Note** makes students aware of potential negative consequences of an action, setting, or decision that are not easily known.
	Display Slide provides a prompt to the instructor to display a specific slide. Display Slides are included in the Instructor Guide only.
	An **Instructor Note** is a comment to the instructor regarding delivery, classroom strategy, classroom tools, exceptions, and other special considerations. Instructor Notes are included in the Instructor Guide only.
	Notes Page indicates a page that has been left intentionally blank for students to write on.
	A **Student Note** provides additional information, guidance, or hints about a topic or task.
	A **Version Note** indicates information necessary for a specific version of software.

Course Requirements and Setup

You can find a list of hardware and software requirements to run this class as well as detailed classroom setup procedures in the course files that are available on the CD-ROM that shipped with this book. If your course manual did not come with a CD-ROM, please go to **http://www.elementk.com/courseware-file-downloads** to download the files.

1 Getting Started with Microsoft Office 2010

Lesson Time: 30 minutes

Lesson Objectives:

In this lesson, you will identify the new and enhanced features that are common to all applications in the Microsoft Office suite.

You will:

● Customize the user interface.

● Work with Ribbon tabs.

● Save files in different formats.

● Print files.

Introduction

You worked with earlier versions of Microsoft Office to create documents, spreadsheets, reports, and presentations, and exchange mail messages. The user-friendly interface and enhanced features of Microsoft Office 2010 are designed to streamline your work and maximize productivity. In this lesson, you will identify the redesigned user interface components and changes to file formats in Microsoft Office 2010.

Lets assume that your workstations are upgraded to the latest release of the Microsoft suite of Office applications, the Office 2010. The purpose of any upgrades is to increase efficiency so that users can work with different applications easily. You would, therefore, want to familiarize yourself with the features of Office 2010 to take full advantage of the suite.

TOPIC A

Customize the User Interface

You are familiar with using the Office 2003 suite of applications to perform various tasks. When working with a new and improved version of an application, you need to be able to identify various elements of the enhanced user interface and personalize the interface to suit your preferences. In this topic, you will customize the Microsoft Office 2010 user interface.

While working with new software, you could potentially waste a significant amount of time searching for specific options in the work environment. You can prevent this by familiarizing yourself with the elements of the user interface. This will help you achieve the output that you are seeking with reduction in time and efficiency when working on office tasks.

The Microsoft Office [Application] User Interface

In Microsoft Office 2010, major interface elements such as the *Ribbon, Quick Access* toolbar, and *status bar* are common to all applications.

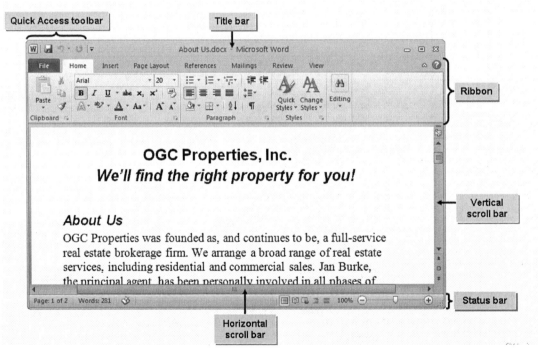

Figure 1-1: The components of the Word 2010 application window.

Interface Element	Description
The Ribbon	A panel at the top portion of an application. It contains several tabs that are organized in the order in which they will be usually needed when working with the application. Each tab contains groups of commands that you may need to work in a file. You can choose to hide the Ribbon to view more content of a file.

Interface Element	Description
The Quick Access toolbar	A toolbar that is displayed at the top of the window, above the Ribbon. It provides easy access to frequently used commands such as **Save, Undo,** and **Repeat.** In addition, you can customize this toolbar to include other commands that you may need based on your preferences. You can also position the Quick Access toolbar below the Ribbon.
The status bar	A frame that is located at the bottom of the application window. It displays a number of tasks relating to an open file's functionality, in a well-organized manner. It also displays information on the file and context information based on the current selection. You can customize the status bar to add or remove displayed information.

Status Bar Display Differences

The status bar in various Office 2010 applications displays different options and information.

Office Application	The Status Bar Displays
Word	The page number of a document, the number of sections, the line and column numbers, a live word count, and a contextual spell checker. The Microsoft Office Status Bar also displays whether the Track Changes mode is turned on or off. You can use the status bar to switch between different views, or to instantaneously zoom the document in or out to any desired size by using the **Zoom** slider. Additionally, the status bar displays the number of authors editing the particular document, and its current upload status. The status bar also provides options for recording macros.
Excel	Information such as the current cell reference, selection modes, page number, average, and sum. It also provides access to the **Macro Record** dialog box. Additionally, you can use the status bar to navigate to the different view modes, or to zoom the spreadsheet in or out.
PowerPoint	The slide number and theme used. You can also use the status bar to navigate to the different view modes, zoom the presentation in or out, and zoom out to fit slide content onto one page. Additionally, it displays the number of authors editing the presentation, and its current upload status.
Access	The current view of a table, report, query, or form. You can also switch between different views by using the status bar.
Outlook	Information about the active folder, quota, filter, reminders, shortcuts, and zoom options.

Shortcut Keys

Office 2003 allowed you to work with the application using various menus and shortcut keys. In Office 2010, menu was deprecated, however, you can still use the same shortcut keys as that of Office 2003 to work with the application.

The Ribbon

The Ribbon organizes commands on different tabs. Each tab is divided into logical groups that contain sets of commands. Each group represents a collection of features designed to perform a specific set of tasks, based on their priority and sequence. The commands in different groups are represented as large and small buttons. The large buttons represent commonly used features, and the smaller buttons represent minor features that are designed to work together with larger buttons to achieve a common result.

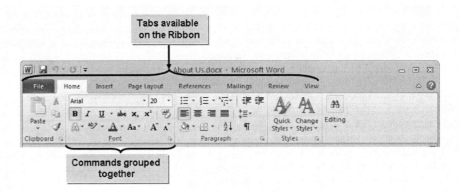

Figure 1-2: The Home tab of the Ribbon displaying commands in various groups.

The Home Tab

The **Home** tab is displayed by default in the Microsoft Office 2010 interface. It generally contains clipboard commands, commands to format text, and various other frequently used formatting options.

Screen Resolutions and the Ribbon

The new user interface is optimized for multiple screen resolutions. As the screen resolution decreases, the groups appear smaller, and as the resolution increases, the groups appear larger. On larger screens, the Ribbon shows larger versions of groups. This means that users with larger monitors will be able to view more details of the options.

Customizable Ribbon Tabs

Office 2010 allows users to customize existing Ribbon tabs and create custom tabs to suit a personal workflow and provide better access to frequently used commands. You can remove the custom tabs when you no longer need them. However, you cannot remove the default tabs from the application, but you do have the option of hiding them.

Benefits of the Ribbon

You can access most of the commands and options from the Ribbon, which you previously accessed using menus and dialog boxes. The Ribbon helps users to easily identify the desired commands and perform both simple and advanced operations quickly, without having to navigate extensively through the application's interface.

Dialog Box Launchers

Dialog box launchers are small buttons with downward pointing arrows that occupy the bottom-right corner of certain groups on the Ribbon. They launch dialog boxes or task panes with commands that are specific to the features found in that group. These commands are used to adjust the settings that are usually not available on the Ribbon.

The Backstage View

The *Backstage view* in Office 2010 is the interface that is displayed when you select the **File** tab. It contains a series of tabs that group similar commands. It also displays the compatibility, permissions, and version information about an Office file. It simplifies access to different features in the application and lets you save, share, print, and publish files with a few mouse clicks.

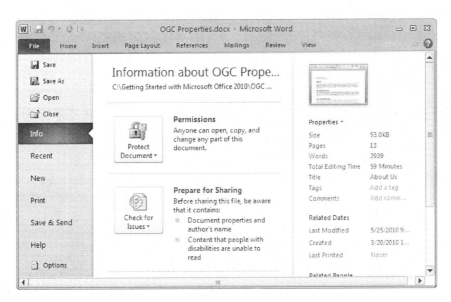

Figure 1-3: *The Backstage view displaying the options on the File tab.*

The [Application] Options Dialog Box

The **[Application] Options** dialog box contains a series of tabs, each with commands required to customize specific elements of the application.

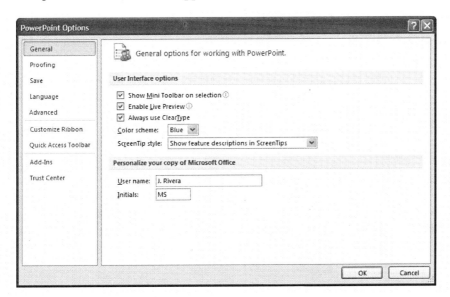

Figure 1-4: *The tabs available in the PowerPoint Options dialog box.*

Tab	Allows You To
General	Personalize the work environment by setting options such as the color scheme, user name, and ScreenTip style. There is also an option to enable the Live Preview feature. In Excel, you can specify options for new workbooks. In Outlook, options in the **Start up options** section allow you to specify whether Outlook should be the default program for mails, contacts, and calendars. In Access, you can specify options for new databases. In PowerPoint, you can specify options to work with the various user interface elements. This tab is present in Access, Word, Excel, Outlook, and PowerPoint.
Proofing	Customize various options to set the AutoCorrect, spelling, and formatting settings. You can specify options for how textual content should be corrected and formatted. You can also choose settings to ignore certain words or spelling errors in certain files.

Contextual spelling checks and evaluates words contextually to catch more spelling errors. Options allow you to include words from other languages such as French and Spanish. This tab is present in Word, Excel, and PowerPoint. |
Save	Specify the customization options for saving documents. Depending on how often you want to save the backup information of a file, you can specify the frequency at which the file will be auto saved. This tab is present in Word, Excel, Outlook, Access, and PowerPoint
Language	Modify Office language preferences. This tab is present in Word, Excel, Outlook, Access, and PowerPoint.
Advanced	Specify advanced options for editing, formatting, displaying, calculating, presenting, printing, saving, and accessing options for files. This tab is present in Word, Excel, Outlook, and PowerPoint.
Customize Ribbon	Customize the Ribbon and shortcut options. Using this tab, you can select tabs that you want added to the Ribbon and hide the ones that you do not need. This tab is present in Word, Excel, Outlook, Access, and PowerPoint.
Quick Access Toolbar	Customize the Quick Access toolbar. Using this tab, you can select the commands that you want added to the Quick Access toolbar. You can also opt to position the Quick Access toolbar below the Ribbon. This tab is present in Word, Excel, Outlook, Access, and PowerPoint.
Add-Ins	Manage Office add-ins if you are using extensions to enhance Office applications. Extensions are add-ins that introduce new functionality to an application. This tab is present in Word, Excel, Outlook, Access, and PowerPoint.
Trust Center	Secure the system and files. Using the **Advanced Trust Center Settings** button on this tab, you can set security measures needed to keep a file secure. This tab is present in Word, Excel, Outlook, Access, and PowerPoint.

ScreenTips

A *ScreenTip* is a label that appears when the mouse pointer is placed over a tool, describing the task that can be performed using the tool. ScreenTips replace the tooltips that were used in Office 2003 and earlier versions and help users to identify the functionality of the commands and options that they are not familiar with. You can customize a ScreenTip on the **General** tab of the **[Application] Options** dialog box to display the level of detail that you want to display in ScreenTips.

Application Specific Tabs

In addition to other Office interface tabs, the **[Application] Options** dialog box provides a few more tabs that can be used to customize options that are specific to each application.

Application	*Tab Description*
Word	The **Display** tab contains options to modify how text is displayed on screen and in print. You can opt to show or hide certain page elements such as highlights, formatting marks, and ScreenTips.
Excel	The **Formulas** tab contains options to change options related to formula calculation, performance, and error handling.
Outlook	• The **Mail** tab provides options to change the settings for messages that you create and receive. • The **Calendar** tab contains options to customize the settings for calendars, meetings, and time zones. • The **Contacts** tab contains options to modify how you work with your contacts. • The **Tasks** tab provides options to define how tasks and to-do items are tracked. • The **Notes and Journal** tab enables you to personalize the settings for notes and journal. • The **Search** tab provides options to modify the search process. • The **Mobile** tab contains options to define how Outlook items will be synchronized with mobile devices.
Access	• The **Current Database** tab contains options to change options for the current database. • The **Datasheet** tab contains options to customize the way datasheets look in Access. • The **Object Designers** tab provides options to define the default settings of data objects. • The **Client Settings** tab provides options to change the way the client behaves.

The Mini Toolbar

The *Mini toolbar* is a floating toolbar that is displayed when you select text. It consists of commonly used text formatting options, and includes commands for the font, size, color, format painter, style, and text alignment. The Mini toolbar disappears when you deselect text.

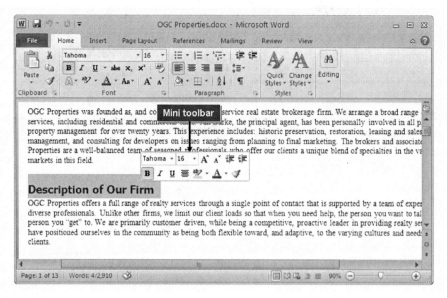

Figure 1-5: *The Mini toolbar displaying the various font formatting options.*

The Mini toolbar is also accessible when you right-click the selected text.

How to Customize the User Interface

Procedure Reference: Create a File

To create a file:

1. Launch the desired Office application.
2. Select the **File** tab and choose **New.**
   - In Word, in the **Available Templates** section, select **Blank document.**
   - In Excel, in the **Available Templates** section, select **Blank workbook.**
   - In PowerPoint, in the **Available Templates and Themes** section, select **Blank presentation.**
   - In Access, in the **Available Templates** section, select **Blank database.**

Procedure Reference: Open a File

To open a file:

1. Launch the desired Office application.
2. Select the **File** tab and choose **Open.**
3. If necessary, in the **Open** dialog box, navigate to the desired location.
4. Select the file and click **Open.**
5. In the **Open** dialog box, navigate to the desired location.
6. Select the file and click **Open.**

Procedure Reference: Save a File

To save a file:

1. Select the **File** tab and choose **Save As.**

2. In the **Save As** dialog box, in the **File name** text box, type the name of the document and click **Save.**

 When saving a file for the first time, the **Save As** dialog box appears even when you click **Save** to enable you to select a location and specify a name for the file.

Procedure Reference: Customize the Microsoft Office 2010 User Interface

To customize the Microsoft Office 2010 user interface:

1. Select the **File** tab and choose **Options.**

2. In the **[Application] Options** dialog box, in the left pane, select the desired tab.

3. In the right pane, modify the desired options.

4. Click **OK** to apply the changes.

Procedure Reference: Customize the Quick Access Toolbar

To customize the Quick Access toolbar:

1. Display the **[Application] Options** dialog box.

   - Click the **File** tab to display the **[Application] Options** dialog box and select the **Quick Access Toolbar** tab or;

   - Click the Customize Quick Access Toolbar drop-down arrow and from the **Customize Quick Access Toolbar** menu, choose **More Commands**.

2. In the **[Application] Options** dialog box, in the right pane, below the **Choose Commands From** section, select the desired command.

3. Click **Add** to add the selected command to the Quick Access toolbar.

4. If necessary, below the **Customize Quick Access Toolbar** section, select the desired command and click **Remove.**

5. If necessary, organize the commands in the **Customize Quick Access Toolbar** section by using the **Move Up, Move Down,** or **Reset** button to set the appearance of commands on the Quick Access toolbar.

6. If necessary, below the **Choose Commands From** section, click **<Separator>** and then click **Add** and use the **Move Up** or **Move Down** button to position the separator.

7. If necessary, check the **Show Quick Access Toolbar below the Ribbon** check box to position the Quick Access toolbar below the Ribbon.

8. Click **OK** to apply the modification to the Quick Access toolbar.

Procedure Reference: Add a Command or Group to the Quick Access Toolbar from the Ribbon

To add a command or group to the Quick Access toolbar from the Ribbon:

1. Select the tab that has the desired command or group.

2. Right-click the desired command or text region in the group and choose **Add To Quick Access Toolbar.**

You can add any number of commands or groups to the Quick Access toolbar. However, the Ribbon cannot be added to the Quick Access toolbar.

Procedure Reference: Customize the Status Bar

To customize the status bar:

1. On the status bar, right-click to display the **Customize Status Bar** menu.
2. Customize the status bar.
   - From the **Customize the Status Bar** menu, choose the required items to add them to the status bar.
   - From the **Customize the Status Bar** menu, choose the required checked items to remove them from the status bar.
3. Click away from the menu to close it.

Procedure Reference: Format Text Using the Mini Toolbar

To format text using the Mini toolbar:

1. Select the text to be formatted to display the Mini toolbar.
2. Move the mouse pointer over the transparent Mini toolbar to make it visible.
3. On the Mini toolbar, click a command button to format the selected text.
4. Move the mouse pointer away from the Mini toolbar or deselect the text to hide the Mini toolbar.

ACTIVITY 1-1

Customizing the Microsoft Word 2010 Interface

Data Files:

C:\084574Data\Getting Started with Microsoft Office 2010\Management.docx

Scenario:

Your company has just installed the Microsoft Office 2010 suite. Because you will be frequently working with the Word application, you decide to spend some time exploring the new user interface elements of the Word application. As you work with Word, you realize that it would be helpful if you have the commands that you intend to use more often in a quickly accessible location for increased efficiency. In addition, you want to personalize the information displayed on the status bar.

---

1. Explore the Word 2010 user interface.

   a. Choose **Start→All Programs→Microsoft Office→Microsoft Word 2010** to launch the Microsoft Word 2010 application.

   b. If necessary, in the **User Name** dialog box, click **OK.**

   c. If necessary, in the **Welcome to Microsoft Office 2010** dialog box, select the **Don't make changes** option and click **OK.**

   d. Select the **File** tab, observe the options on the tab, and then choose **Open.**

   e. In the **Open** dialog box, navigate to the C:\084574Data\Getting Started with Microsoft Office 2010 folder and open the Management.docx file.

   f. On the Quick Access toolbar, hover the mouse pointer over each button to view its ScreenTip.

   g. On the Ribbon, select different tabs to view their commands.

   h. On the status bar, on the right side, hover the mouse pointer over each view button to view the respective ScreenTip.

---

2. Add commands to the Quick Access toolbar.

   a. On the Quick Access toolbar, from the **Customize Quick Access Toolbar** menu, select **New.**

   b. Observe that the **New** button is added to the Quick Access toolbar.

   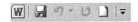

   c. From the **Customize Quick Access Toolbar** menu, select **Open.**

---

    d.   From the **Customize Quick Access Toolbar** menu, select **More Commands.**

    e.   In the **Word Options** dialog box, on the **Quick Access Toolbar** tab, from the **Choose commands from** drop-down list, select **File Tab.**

    f.   Below the **Choose commands from** drop-down list, in the list box, select **Close.**

    g.   Click **Add** and then click **OK** to apply the settings.

    h.   Observe that the **New, Open,** and **Close** buttons are added to the Quick Access toolbar.

3.   Customize the status bar.

    a.   Right-click the blank space on the status bar to display the **Customize Status Bar** menu.

    b.   Observe that a check mark is displayed against the **Page Number** option, indicating that the option is displayed on the status bar.

    c.   From the **Customize Status Bar** menu, choose **Section** to add it to the status bar.

    d.   Observe that the section information is added to the status bar.

    e.   Similarly, add **Line Number** to the status bar.

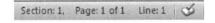

    f.   Click away from the status bar to close the **Customize Status Bar** menu.

4.   Format text using the Mini toolbar.

    a.   Triple-click the bold formatted text "Relocation Services."

    b.   Observe that the transparent Mini toolbar appears beside the text "Relocation Services."

    c.   Hover the mouse pointer over the transparent Mini toolbar to make the Mini toolbar clearly visible.

    d.   On the Mini toolbar, click the **Italic** button.

e. From the **Font Size** drop-down list, select **14.**

f. Click outside the selected text to view the changes.

g. Select the **File** tab and choose **Save As.**

h. In the **Save as** dialog box, in the **File name** text box, type *My Management.docx* and click the **Save** button.

i. On the Quick Access toolbar, click the **Close** button.

TOPIC B
Work with Ribbon Tabs

You customized the Office 2010 user interface. Unlike the regular interface commands, certain commands and options are available on the Ribbon contextually when specific objects such as tables, charts, and graphics are selected. In this topic, you will work with Ribbon tabs.

Imagine a workspace where you have all the tools, buttons, and options displayed in the interface. Searching for a specific option is like searching for that one piece of paper in an overstuffed file cabinet. Office 2010 provides you with a set of contextual command tabs that appear only when relevant object types are selected. This facility provides you with an uncluttered workspace and ensures quick access to relevant commands for editing and formatting specific objects, similar locating books in a library.

Contextual Tabs

Contextual tabs are specialized tabs that are displayed when a specific type of object is selected. They are displayed next to the core Ribbon tabs. You can switch between contextual tabs and core tabs as needed. Because they are context based, so the scope of their commands and tools is restricted to only the objects for which they appear. When you deselect the object, the respective contextual tabs disappear.

Figure 1-6: The Picture Tools Format contextual tab displaying options to format a picture.

Types of Contextual Tabs

Office 2010 provides several types of contextual tabs to access commands that are relevant to an object. The groups and commands in each of the contextual tabs vary based on the object type.

Contextual Tab	Description
Format	This tab is displayed when you select pictures, shapes, charts, SmartArt graphics, clip art, reports, forms, or sound and movie clips. The commands on this tab can be used to format the selected object. You can change the object's style, modify its color or size, or change its position. You can also remove the background in a picture, make color corrections, add artistic effects, and trim videos. In Access 2010, it provides commands to format forms and reports.

Contextual Tab	Description
Design	This tab is displayed when you select tables, charts, reports, forms, or SmartArt graphics. The commands on this tab can be used to make changes to design elements, such as the style and appearance of the object.
Layout	This tab is displayed when you select tables and charts. The commands on this tab can be used to change the layout of the existing chart or table by merging, splitting, inserting, or deleting elements.
Playback	This tab is displayed when you insert media clips such as sound and movie. The commands on this tab can be used to adjust the volume, edit and preview a sound or movie clip, add bookmarks, and specify playback options.

Contextual Tab Groups

Contextual tab groups are sets of contextual tabs that appear in Office 2010 based on the selected object in an application.

Contextual Tab Group	Description
Table Tools	This group allows you to set various properties of an inserted table and apply different styles to it. It consists of the **Design** and **Layout** tabs.
Picture Tools	This group contains options that allow you to modify a picture on the **Format** contextual tab.
Drawing Tools	This group is used to insert shapes such as rectangles, circles, lines, arrows, callouts, and flow chart symbols. You can edit existing WordArt text, increase or decrease word spacing, pick alternate styles, and add effects.
Chart Tools	This group is used to insert a chart and compare its data. It consists of the **Design, Layout,** and **Format** tabs.
SmartArt Tools	This group is used to insert a SmartArt graphic to communicate information visually. It consists of the **Design** and **Format** tabs.
Equation Tools	This group is used to insert common mathematical equations or to build equations by using the library. It consists of the **Design** tab, which provides options to insert common mathematical equations and symbols and to add some additional features such as fractions, radices, integrals, and matrices to the equation.
Header & Footer Tools	This group is used to insert and customize the header and footer sections. It consists of the **Design** tab. You can customize the header and footer sections by selecting the header and footer styles from their respective galleries. You can also add details such as date, time, page numbers, and images, among others. You can align and position them on select pages, as desired. Within this tab, you can also switch between headers and footers to make modifications to the elements within them.
Audio Tools	This group is used to insert and edit audio clips in a file. It consists of the **Format** and **Playback** tabs.
Video Tools	This group is used to insert and edit video clips in a file. It consists of the **Format** and **Playback** tabs.

Additional Application Specific Contextual Tabs

Office 2010 provides additional application specific contextual tabs that allow you to use specific features of that application.

Application	Description
Word	The **Ink Tools** tab allows you to highlight text, draw shapes, erase ink strokes, and convert ink drawings into shapes. This tab is also available in PowerPoint.
Excel	The **PivotTable Tools** tab allows you to count, sort, and calculate the total data stored in a table or spreadsheet and create a pivot table displaying the summarized data. The **Sparkline Tools** tab allows you to edit *Sparklines* in a spreadsheet.
Access	• The **Form Design Tools** tab allows you to design various forms in a database. • The **Report Layout Tools** tab allows you to change the settings of reports created based on the forms created in Excel. • The **Query Tools** tab allows you to change settings related to queries. • The **Arrange** tab is displayed when you insert or open a form or report in Microsoft Access. It contains commands to set the layout of a form or report. • The **Page Setup** tab is displayed when you open a report in Microsoft Access. It contains commands to set the page size and layout of a report.
Outlook	• The **Calendar Tools** tab allows you to make adjustments to the appointment details and arrange various appointments. • The **Task Tools** tab allows you to set tasks and make adjustments to the tasks set. • The **Attachment Tools** tab allows you to add attachments to your tasks and appointments.
PowerPoint	The **CD Audio Tools** tab allows you to insert and edit audio clips from a CD.

Galleries

A *gallery* is a repository for elements that belong to the same category. It acts as a central location for accessing various styles and appearance settings of an object. Galleries provide you with a set of visual choices to enhance the look and feel of elements while working on a document. Office 2010 provides galleries for various options such as styles, shapes, and text effects. You can choose from any of the preset formats and styles to quickly alter an object in a file.

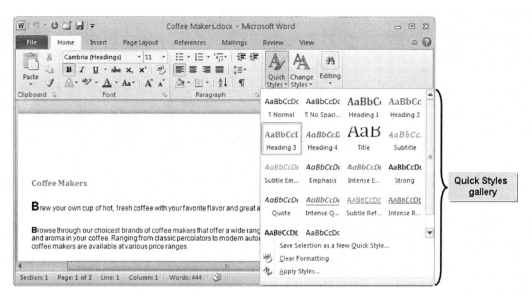

Figure 1-7: The Quick Styles gallery displaying various styles.

 Some gallery options are also available on shortcut menus that can be accessed by a simple right-click. These options allow users to quickly access the relevant galleries.

The Live Preview Feature

Live Preview is a feature that enables you to preview the results of applying design and formatting changes to a document, without actually applying them. These changes are displayed in the document when you hover the mouse pointer over the available options in a gallery.

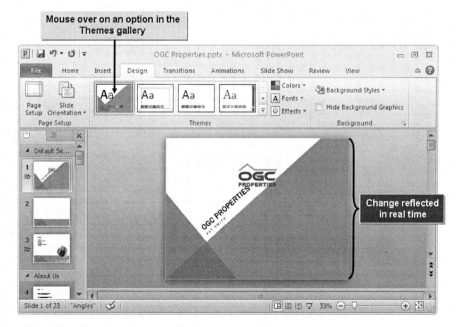

Figure 1-8: The Live Preview feature displaying real-time changes.

Paste Preview Options

Office 2010 provides several options to paste content from the Clipboard. These options are displayed based on the content copied into the Clipboard. The paste option can be accessed from the **Paste** drop-down list on the **Home** tab or from the right-click context menu. You can hover the mouse pointer over a paste option to view a live preview of that option.

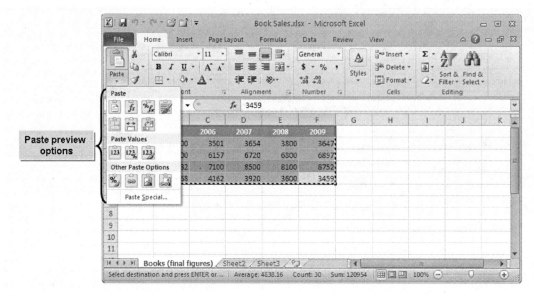

Figure 1-9: The paste preview options available in a spreadsheet.

How to Work with Ribbon Tabs

Procedure Reference: Format Objects Using Contextual Tabs

To format an object using contextual tabs:

1. Select the object to be formatted to display the contextual tabs.

2. From the displayed contextual tab, apply the desired format commands.

3. Deselect the object to hide the contextual tabs.

ACTIVITY 1-2
Working with the Contextual Tabs

Data Files:

C:\084574Data\Getting Started with Microsoft Office 2010\OGC Description.docx

Before You Begin:

The Word 2010 application is open.

Scenario:

With the page border and consistent line spacing applied, the OGC Description.docx document looks quite formal. You are now ready to hand off the document to your manager for approval. Upon a final check, you realize that you have not added a header to the document.

---

1. Insert a header.

    a. On the Quick Access toolbar, click the **Open** button.

    b. In the **Open** dialog box, navigate to the C:\084574Data\Getting Started with Microsoft Office 2010 folder and open the OGC Description.docx file.

    c. Select the **Insert** tab, and in the **Header & Footer** group, click the **Header** drop-down arrow.

    d. From the displayed gallery, in the **Built-In** section, scroll down and select **Mod (Odd Page).**

    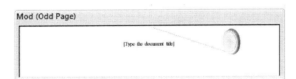

    e. Observe that a header is inserted in the document and the **Design** contextual tab is displayed on the **Header & Footer Tools** tool tab on the Ribbon.

    f. In the **Header** section, select the text "About Us".

    g. Select the **Home** tab, in the **Font** group, click the **Bold** button.

    h. On the **Home** tab, and in the **Font** group, from the **Font Size** drop-down list, select **18.**

    i. Click outside the selected text to view the changes.

    j. In the header section, select the "About Us" text again.

k.   Type **WELCOME TO OGC PROPERTIES**

2.   Format the header using contextual tabs.

a.   At the top-right corner of the header, select the image.

b.   Observe that the **Format** contextual tab is displayed on the **Drawing Tools** tool tab on the Ribbon.

c.   Select the **Format** contextual tab, and in the **Shape Styles** group, click the **More** button to view the gallery.

d.   From the displayed gallery, select the **Subtle Effect - Aqua, Accent 5** option, which is the sixth option in the fourth row.

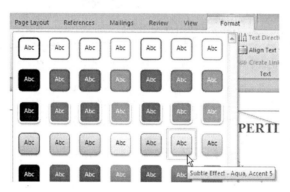

e.   Select the **Header & Footer Tools Design** contextual tab, and in the **Close** group, click **Close Header and Footer.**

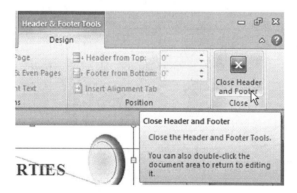

3.   Save and close the document.

a.   Select the **File** tab and choose **Save As.**

b.   In the **Save As** dialog box, in the **File name** text box, type *My OGC Description.docx* and click **Save.**

c.   On the Quick Access toolbar, click **Close.**

d.   Select the **File** tab and choose **Exit.**

TOPIC C
Save Files in Different Formats

You worked with Ribbon tabs to add effects to content in files. In addition to knowing how to work in the interface, it is essential to be able to save, retrieve, and share information. In this topic, you will save files in different formats to share content.

Sharing information with your colleagues, senior officials, and clients is an integral part of working in a corporate world. When dealing with different clients, you need to ensure that your documents are compatible with their applications. However, creating compatible documents in compatible formats can be a daunting and time-consuming task. Office 2010 allows you to save a file in different formats for easy integration with other applications and platforms.

The XML File Format

Office 2010 uses *XML* as the default file format to save files. The XML format is a compact and robust file format that enables easy integration of Office 2010 files with other applications and platforms.

Application	Description
Word	Word 2010 provides a varied list of file formats: ● Word document (.docx) is the default Office Word 2010 file format. ● Word macro-enabled document (.docm) is the default Word 2010 file format for macro-enabled documents. It uses the same basic XML format as the Word 2010 XML document format, but can store VBA macro code. ● Word template (.dotx) is the default format for a Word template. It is created while saving document styles and formatting. ● Word macro-enabled template (.dotm) is the default format for a Word macro-enabled template. Word 2010 stores macro code for use with other Word documents. By default, documents are saved as .docx files even when created from a Word 2010 XML macro-enabled template.
Excel	Excel 2010 provides a varied list of file formats: ● Excel workbook (.xlsx) is the default Excel 2010 XML file format. ● Excel macro-enabled workbook (.xlsm) is the XML-based file format that is used to save workbooks with VBA macro code. ● Excel template (.xltx) is the default Excel template file format. ● Excel macro-enabled template (.xltm) is the Excel macro-enabled template format that can contain VBA macro code. ● Excel binary workbook (.xlsb) is the Excel binary file format (BIFF12) that allows the use of VBA projects. ● Excel add-in (.xlam) is an XML-based macro-enabled supplemental program that runs additional code and allows the use of VBA projects.

Application	Description
PowerPoint	PowerPoint 2010 provides a varied list of file formats: • PowerPoint presentation (.pptx) is the default PowerPoint XML format. • PowerPoint macro-enabled presentation (.pptm) is also a basic XML format like the .pptx format, but can store VBA macro code. • PowerPoint template (.potx) is an XML-based PowerPoint template. • PowerPoint macro-enabled template (.potm) is an XML-based PowerPoint template that can store VBA macro code. • PowerPoint show (.ppsx) is an XML-based PowerPoint slide show that runs automatically when opened. • PowerPoint macro-enabled show (.ppsm) is an XML-based slide show that runs automatically when opened and contains VBA macro code. • PowerPoint add-in (.ppam) is an XML-based macro-enabled presentation that is run as a supplemental program.
Access	Access 2010 provides a varied list of file formats: • Access database (.accdb) is the default Access database format. It supports features such as multi-value fields and attachments. • Access executable (.accde) is an executable file format and it replaces the .mde file format that was available in previous versions of Access. • Access template (.accdt) is the file format for database templates. • Access runtime (.accdr) is the file format for runtime files.

 The "x" in Office 2010 file extensions stands for XML.

Advantages of XML File Formats

Office 2010 uses XML as the default file format. XML formats can have multiple advantages.

Advantage	Description
Smaller file size	These new formats use zip compression to reduce file size by as much as 75%. They reduce the disk space required to store files and the bandwidth used to share documents across networks.
Improved information recovery	The files saved in these new formats are modularly structured. Different data components in the files are stored separately. Therefore, the files can be opened even if a component within the files are damaged or corrupted.
Easier detection of documents with macros	These new file formats with their distinct file name extensions make it easy to distinguish files that contain macros, from those that do not. File extensions ending with "x" cannot contain VBA macros or ActiveX controls, whereas file extensions ending with "m" can.

Inter Conversion of Access Databases in Different Formats

When working with databases created in previous versions of Access, you can use the **Convert** option available in the Backstage view to upgrade the databases to the Access 2010 file format. However, to save the latest *.accdb database format in the *.mdb file format, the database must not include any of the enhanced features that are available in Access 2010.

Easy Identification of Macro-Enabled Files

It is very easy to identify a file in Office 2010 that contains macros. Any file type extension ending with "m" contains macro codes.

The Compatibility Checker Feature

The *Compatibility Checker feature* in Word 2010 allows you to check different document formats for compatibility when they are saved in an earlier version of Word.

Compatibility Method	Description
Convert a document to an earlier version	You can use the **Convert** option to convert a document saved in an earlier version of Word to the Word 2010 file format.
Save as an earlier version	You can save a document that is saved in the DOCX format, in a file format that is compatible with earlier versions of Word. In the **Save As** dialog box, select the document type for the appropriate version of Word.
Check compatibility	You can use the **Microsoft Word Compatibility Checker** dialog box to check for any compatibility issue in a document.

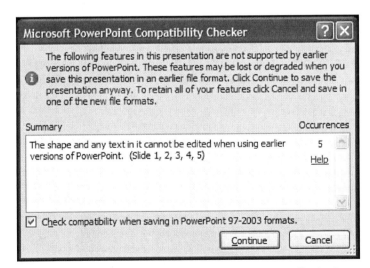

Figure 1-10: The Compatibility Checker feature displaying compatibility issues.

The PDF and XPS File Formats

Using Microsoft Office 2010, you can publish any Microsoft Office files in the Portable Document Format (PDF) or in the XML Paper Specification (XPS) file format. The PDF or XPS file format is a fixed-layout electronic format that preserves the file format exactly as intended, both in the print and online views. These formats are used extensively to share information because they ensure that the file contents cannot be easily edited.

How to Save Files in Different Formats

Procedure Reference: Upgrade a File to the XML File Format

To upgrade a file to the XML file format:

1. In Office 2010, open a file saved in an earlier version of Office.
2. Select the **File** tab and choose **Save As.**
3. If necessary, in the **Save As** dialog box, navigate to the desired location to save the file.
4. From the **Save as type** drop-down list, select the XML file format in which you want to save the file.
5. Click **Save.**

Procedure Reference: Save a File in the File Format of an Earlier Version

To save a file in the file format of an earlier version:

1. Open an Office 2010 file.
2. Select the **File** tab and choose **Save As.**
3. If necessary, in the **Save As** dialog box, navigate to the desired location to save the file.
4. From the **Save as type** drop-down list, select **[Application] 97–2003 [File Type] [Extension].**
5. Click **Save** to save the file in the file format of the earlier version.
6. If necessary, in the **Microsoft [Application] Compatibility Checker** dialog box, on the title bar, next to the close button, click the help button to obtain help to resolve compatibility issues.
7. In the **Microsoft [Application] Compatibility Checker** dialog box, click **Continue** to modify the features that are not supported in the earlier version.

ACTIVITY 1-3
Saving a Presentation

Data Files:

C:\084574Data\Getting Started with Microsoft Office 2010\Company Introduction.pptx

Scenario:

You want to send a copy of the presentation's content for your manager's review. Because your manager does not have Office suite installed, you decide to send the presentation in the PDF format. You also intend to work from home next week and, therefore, want to save the presentation to your laptop. You need to save the presentation in the PowerPoint 2003 format because you do not have Office 2010 installed on your laptop. You also need all the objects to appear correctly in the earlier PowerPoint format when you work on the presentation at home.

---

1. Save the presentation in the PDF format.

   a. Choose **Start→All Programs→Microsoft Office→Microsoft PowerPoint 2010** to launch the Microsoft PowerPoint 2010 application.

   b. Select the **File** tab and choose **Open.**

   c. In the **Open** dialog box, navigate to the C:\084574Data\Getting Started with Microsoft Office 2010 folder and open the Company Introduction.pptx file.

   d. Select the **File** tab and choose **Save As.**

   e. In the **Save As** dialog box, in the **File name** text box, type *My Company Introduction*

   f. In the **Save as type** drop-down list, select **PDF(*.pdf)** and click **Save.**

---

2. View the My Company Introduction PDF file.

   a. Observe that the Acrobat Reader automatically opens the presentation as soon as it is saved.

   b. Scroll down and view the contents of the presentation in the PDF format.

   c. Close the My Company Introduction.pdf file.

---

3. Save the presentation in an earlier version of PowerPoint.

   a. Select the **File** tab and choose **Save As.**

   b. In the **Save As** dialog box, in the **File name** text box, type *My Company Introduction 2003.pptx*

   c. From the **Save as type** drop-down list, select **PowerPoint 97–2003 Presentation (*.ppt)** and click **Save.**

   d. In the **Microsoft PowerPoint Compatibility Checker** dialog box, observe that the objects that are not compatible with the PPT file format are summarized and click **Continue.**

When you click **Continue,** the compatibility issues will be fixed before saving the file.

e. Observe that the title bar displays the text "[Compatibility Mode]" after the file name and close the presentation.

f. Close the application.

TOPIC D
Print Files

You saved a file to different formats to enable easy sharing. You may also want a printed copy of the document. But before you print the document, it is smart to preview it and check to ensure that it looks the way you intended it to look on the printed page. In this topic, you will preview and print Office 2010 files.

When you design a presentation in PowerPoint, providing hard copies of the document to the audience allows them to follow the information you are presenting more effectively. It also provides them with a place to jot down any notes to use as reference material after the presentation.

Print Options in the Backstage View

The **Print** option in Office 2010 is integrated into the Backstage view. It is divided into two panes. The left pane is used to specify options, such as print, printer, and settings, which allow you to select a printer from the available list of printers, modify settings such as page orientation, paper size, margin properties, and print files. The right pane displays a preview of the file and also contains the **Zoom** slider and options to view the next and previous pages. You can also specify print settings in the **Print** dialog box that can be launched by pressing **Ctrl+p.**

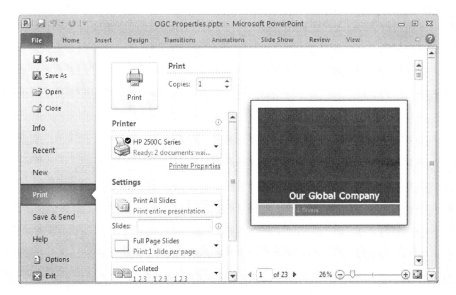

Figure 1-11: The Print section displaying the preview of a slide in a presentation.

How to Print Files

Procedure Reference: Preview and Print an Office File

To preview and print an Office file:

1. Select the **File** tab and choose **Print.**

2. In left pane, choose the printer and apply print settings.

    ● In the **Printer** section, from the drop-down list, select a printer.

    ● In the **Settings** section, specify the print settings.

3. In the right pane, view a preview of the file to be printed.

4. In the **Print** section, in the **Copies** text box, enter the number of copies you want to print and click **Print.**

ACTIVITY 1-4
Printing a Word Document

Data Files:

C:\084574Data\Getting Started with Microsoft Office 2010\OGC Properties.docx

Scenario:

Your document is ready for delivery. You want to print the document and the main text of each page for reference. However, you need to check whether the paper size and page orientation are set to ensure that the print output is perfect. Your manager has informed you that the document will be included as an appendix in the company's annual report. Therefore, you decide to print the pages of the document to append them to the report.

1. Set the page orientation and paper size of the document.

    a. Choose **Start→All Programs→Microsoft Office→Microsoft Word 2010** to launch the Microsoft Word 2010 application.

    b. On the Quick Access toolbar, click **Open.**

    c. In the **Open** dialog box, navigate to the C:\084574Data\Getting Started with Microsoft Office 2010 folder and open the OGC Properties.docx file.

    d. Select the **File** tab and choose **Print.**

    e. In the **Settings** pane, from the **Portrait Orientation** drop-down list, select **Landscape Orientation.**

    f. In the **Settings** pane, from the **Letter** drop-down list, select **A4.**

2. Preview and print the pages of the document.

    a. In the right pane, preview the setting changes made to the document.

    b. In the **Settings** section, in the first drop-down list, verify that **Print All Pages** is selected.

    c. In the **Print** section, click **Print** to print the pages.

    d. Select the **File** tab and choose **Save As.**

    e. In the **Save As** dialog box, in the **File name** text box, type *My OGC Properties.docx* and click **Save.**

f.   On the Quick Access toolbar, click **Close.**

Lesson 1 Follow-up

In this lesson, you identified the new components of the Office 2010 user interface and the new file formats for saving files. You also customized the Office 2010 environment to suit your requirements. This knowledge and experience will enable you to personalize the workspace, streamline your tasks, and work more efficiently with the new versions of the Office applications.

1. **What do you think are the advantages of the new user interface?**

2. **How will you access the new formatting options in Office 2010?**

2 | Modifying Documents Using Microsoft Word 2010

Lesson Time: 1 hour(s)

Lesson Objectives:

In this lesson, you will modify documents using Microsoft Word 2010.

You will:

- Navigate and find information.
- Apply text styles.
- Add SmartArt graphics.
- Insert screenshots.
- Compare reviewed documents.

Introduction

You identified the different features in the new user interface where commands are organized into various groups on the Ribbon and contextual tabs. Word 2010 has additional options for the appropriate use of font styles and graphics and the reusability of frequently appearing chunks of information. In this lesson, you will modify documents using Microsoft Word 2010.

Whether you are preparing a report for your boss or a proposal for a client, creating a multi-page document is invariably a tedious task. Therefore, while working on official documents, it is crucial to include a cover page, and at times, it is also crucial to create visual elements that enhance the visual appeal of the document. You may also have to maintain standard formatting across different documents. Word 2010, with its simple commands and galleries, helps you create documents that reach the target audience in the proposed manner.

TOPIC A
Navigate and Find Information

You familiarized yourself with the new user interface and its various commands. You are now ready to access information in a document and organize its content. In this topic, you will navigate within a document and restructure information using the Navigation pane.

Search engines make it easy and convenient to locate information on the web. Similarly, the Navigation pane in Word 2010 makes it easy to access content in a document and enables you to navigate across sections, regardless of the length of the document. You no longer need to browse through numerous pages in the document to go to a particular section.

The Navigation Pane

The **Navigation** pane provides you with multiple ways to view and access information in a document. You can navigate to a particular section or a page directly by clicking the corresponding section name or thumbnail of the page.

 The **Navigation** pane also contains improved search features to search for information in a document.

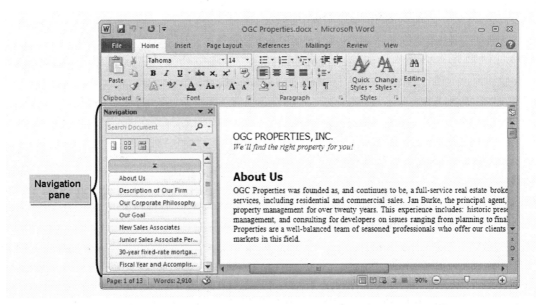

Figure 2-1: The Navigation pane used to navigate through a document and restructure it.

Tab	Description
Browse the headings in your document	Used to view the structure of a document based on the headings and subheadings used in it. You can click a section name in the **Navigation** pane to navigate to that section in a document.

Tab	Description
Browse the pages in your document	Used to view the thumbnail images of pages in a document and navigate to a specific page by clicking the corresponding thumbnail.
Browse the results of your current search	Used to view the results of the searched information. You can click a specific search item in the result to navigate to the location in the document where the searched information was found.

Modifying the Structure of Documents Using the Navigation Pane

The contents of a document can be organized by dragging a section name in the **Navigation** pane to the desired position. You can also promote or demote a section name to restructure the document.

The Improved Find Experience

Word 2010, with its new improved find experience, not only allows you to search for information, but also highlights all the matches in a document. You can see a list of matches along with a small snippet of the context where the searched information was found. The searched result in the document reduces as you refine your search. Various objects such as graphics, tables, equations, footnotes, endnotes, and comments can also be searched for using the improved find feature.

Figure 2-2: The search result being highlighted.

How to Navigate and Find Information

Procedure Reference: Modify a Document Using the Navigation Pane

To modify a document using the **Navigation** pane:

1. Open a Word document.
2. If necessary, on the **View** tab, in the **Show** group, check the **Navigation Pane** check box.
3. If necessary, click the **Browse the headings in your document** tab to view the headings in a document.
4. Right-click the required heading and modify the structure of the document.

   - Choose **Promote** or **Demote** to modify the heading level.
   - Choose **New Heading Before** or **New Heading After** to insert a new heading at the desired location.
   - Choose **New Subheading** to insert a new subheading in the selected section.
   - Choose **Delete** to remove the section.

5. Click and drag a heading and place it at the desired position in the **Navigation** pane to reposition the headings in a document.

Procedure Reference: Search for Information Using the Navigation Pane

To search for information using the **Navigation** pane:

1. Select the **Browse the results from your current search** tab, and in the **Search Document** text box, type the search keyword.
2. In the **Navigation** pane, select a search result to view its occurrence in the document.
3. If necessary, beside the **Search Document** text box, click the drop-down arrow and select **Advanced Find,** and in the **Find and Replace** dialog box, specify the advanced search parameters.
4. In the **Search Document** text box, type the word you want to search, and on the **Browse the pages in your document** tab, select the page that suits your search.

ACTIVITY 2-1
Using the Navigation Pane

Data Files:

C:\084574Data\Modifying Documents\Annual Report.docx

Before You Begin:
The Word 2010 application is open.

Scenario:
You are working on a lengthy report with content that is structured using headings and sub-headings. Within the limited time allotted for the task, you need to quickly navigate through the document and modify its structure by manipulating the outline and headings.

---

1. Restructure the content using the **Navigation** pane.

    a. On the Quick Access toolbar, click the **Open** button.

    b. In the **Open** dialog box, navigate to the C:\084574Data\Modifying Documents folder and open the Annual Report.docx file.

    c. Verify that the **Navigation** pane is displayed.

     If the Navigation pane is not displayed, then on the **View** tab, in the **Show** section, check the **Navigation Pane** check box to display it.

    d. In the Navigation pane, under the "Long-Term Strategy" heading, under the "Invest-ment" heading, right-click the "National Affiliate Program" subheading.

    e. Choose **Show Heading Levels.**

    f.   Observe that the **Show Heading 3** option is selected indicating that all headings upto level 3 headings are displayed in the Navigation panel.

    g.   From the contextual menu, choose **Promote** to change the heading level to level 2.

    h.   Observe that the "National Affiliate Program" heading is promoted to a higher heading level.

    i.   Click and drag the "To Our Stockholders" heading and place it above the "Markets Forecast" heading to restructure the heading.

2.   Modify the content under the "National Affiliate Program" subheading.

    a.   In the **Navigation** pane, click the "National Affiliate Program" subheading to navigate to and view the content under the heading in the document.

    b.   In the first paragraph, toward the end of the third line, double-click **"17"** and type *19*

3.   Search for the word "Company" and locate it.

    a.   In the **Navigation** pane, select the **Browse the results from your current search** tab, and in the **Search Document** text box, click and type *Company*

    b.   In the **Navigation** pane, select the fourth result to view the relevant text in the document.

    c.   Save the document as *My Annual Report.docx*

    d.   On the Quick Access toolbar, click the **Close** button.

TOPIC B
Apply Text Styles

You used the Navigation pane to navigate through a document and modify its structure. You are now ready to begin authoring content. In the course of your work, you may want to make a word, line, or paragraph stand out from the surrounding text. In this topic, you will apply text styles.

When you create a document, you may want to apply a specific set of font styles to text. Instead of accessing each of these options from different dialog boxes, Word 2010 makes it convenient for you to select the desired output from the selections in the preset style galleries and allows you to view the changes that will happen before you set the style. Word 2010 styles help you quickly achieve consistent and customized design and formatting effects.

The Quick Styles Command

The *Quick Styles* command contains sets of styles packaged together to apply design and formatting changes to text in a document. You can select a text style from the **Quick Styles** gallery on the **Home** tab, or from the corresponding galleries of other style commands on the **Design** or **Format** contextual tab available on the **Drawing Tools** tab. You can also modify an existing style or build a new style and add it to the **Quick Styles** gallery.

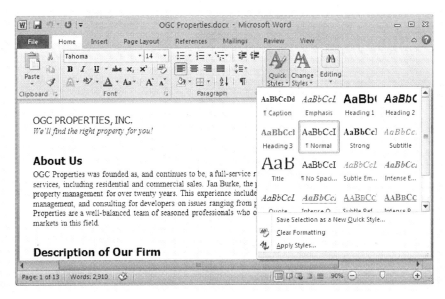

Figure 2-3: Various text styles displayed in the Quick Styles gallery.

The Themes Command

The *Themes* command helps you change the overall design of a document to improve its visual appeal. The **Themes** drop-down list on the **Page Layout** tab contains a set of predefined themes that can be applied to a document. The appearance of objects, such as text, tables, charts, and SmartArt, changes based on the applied theme. You can change the color, fonts, and effects of themes to suit your requirements.

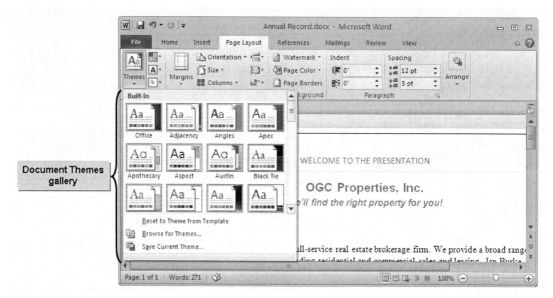

Figure 2-4: The Document Themes gallery displaying the available themes.

New Text Effects

The **Text Effects** command allows you to change the effects of selected text in a document. The **Text Effects** gallery in the **Font** group consists of a set of predefined text styles that can be applied to text to enhance the visual appeal of the document. Text effects that can be applied to text include **Outline, Shadow, Reflection,** and **Glow.**

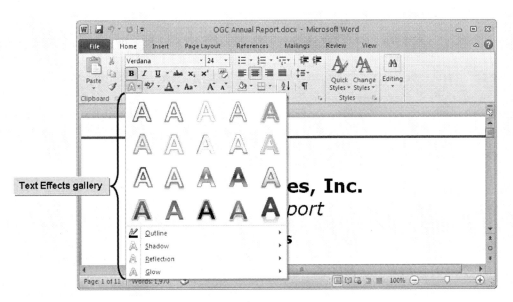

Figure 2-5: *The various text effects available in Word 2010.*

Enhanced WordArt Effects

Word 2010 allows you to increase the visual appeal of text in a document by applying enhanced text effects. *WordArt* allows you to style text with various special effects such as textures, outlines, and styles that are not available through standard font formatting options.

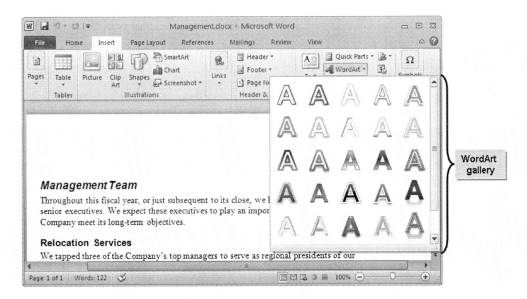

Figure 2-6: *The WordArt gallery displaying the various styles.*

Option	Description
Text Fill	You can fill text with a solid color, gradient, picture, or texture using this option.

Option	Description
Text Outline	You can specify the color, width, and line style for the outline of text using this option.
Text Effects	You can add visual effects to text such as shadow, glow, reflection, and 3D rotation using this option.

Font Styles and Typography

Word 2010 includes new fonts that are designed to improve readability by ensuring that words displayed on screen appear as sharp and clear as those on paper. Calibri, which is a Sans-serif font with soft rounded corners, is the default font in Word 2010. Gabriola is a new font style introduced in Word 2010. OpenType typography, introduced in Word 2010, provides scalable font options to create content in different languages by using typography features such as *ligatures* and *stylistic sets*. The **Grow font** and **Shrink font** buttons allow you to increase or decrease the size of fonts gradually.

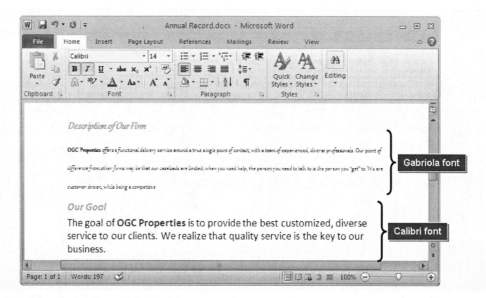

Figure 2-7: *The Gabriola and Calibri fonts used in a document.*

Ligatures are characters made up of two letters combined into one by connecting the letters. Stylistic sets are used to display the same font with a slightly different look in a document. Ligatures are available for some fonts, but they are not enabled by default. You can change the settings for ligatures by using the **Advanced** tab in the **Font** dialog box.

How to Apply Text Styles

Procedure Reference: Create a Quick Style

To create a Quick style:

1. Select the desired text.

2. Apply the desired formatting to the text.

3. Save the formatting as a new style.

   - Right-click the selection and choose **Styles→Save Selection as a New Quick Style** or;

   - On the **Home** tab, in the **Styles** group, click the **More** button, and from the displayed gallery, select **Save Selection as a New Quick Style.**

4. In the **Create New Style from Formatting** dialog box, in the **Name** text box, type a name.

5. Click **OK** to add the style to the **Quick Styles** gallery.

6. If necessary, in the **Styles** group, in the **Quick Styles** gallery, click the **More** button to view the new style.

Procedure Reference: Apply a Text Style from the Quick Styles Gallery

To apply a text style from the **Quick Styles** gallery:

1. Select the text to which you want to apply a style.

2. On the **Home** tab, in the **Styles** group, click the **More** button, and from the **Quick Styles** gallery, select the desired style.

Procedure Reference: Modify an Existing Quick Style

To modify an existing Quick style:

1. On the **Home** tab, in the **Styles** group, in the **Quick Styles** gallery, right-click the desired style and choose **Modify.**

2. In the **Modify Style** dialog box, format the style as needed and click **OK.**

3. If necessary, save the modified style.

   a. On the **Home** tab, in the **Styles** group, from the **Change Styles** drop-down list, hover the mouse over **Style Set** and select **Save as Quick Style Set.**

   b. In the **Save Quick Style Set** dialog box, in the **File name** text box, type a style name and click **Save.**

4. If necessary, click **Change Styles,** and from the **Style Set** drop-down list, select **Reset Document Quick Styles** to restore the default styles.

Procedure Reference: Apply a Document Theme

To apply a document theme:

1. Open the document to which you want to apply a document theme.

2. Select the **Page Layout** tab, and in the **Themes** group, click the **Themes** drop-down arrow to display the Themes gallery.

3. From the Themes gallery, select a predefined theme you want to apply to a document.

4. In the **Themes** group, select an option.

- From the **Theme Fonts** drop-down list, select an option to customize the fonts in the document.
- From the **Theme Effects** drop-down list, select an option to customize the theme effects in the document.
- From the **Theme Colors** drop-down list, select an option to customize the colors in the document.

Procedure Reference: Apply Text Effects in a Document

To apply text effects in a document:

1. Select the text to which you want to apply text effects.
2. On the **Home** tab, in the **Font** group, click the **Text Effects** drop-down arrow to display the Text Effects gallery.
3. From the Text Effects gallery, select an option to apply text effects.
   - Select the predefined text style you want to apply to the text.
   - Select **Outline** and select a color to add colors to the outline of text.
   - Select **Shadow** and select a shadow style to apply shadow styles to text.
   - Select **Reflection** and select a reflection style to apply a reflection style to text.
   - Select **Glow** and select a glow style to apply a glow style to text.

Procedure Reference: Apply WordArt to Text in a Document

To apply WordArt to text in a document:

1. Select the **Insert** tab, and in the **Text** group, click the **WordArt** drop-down arrow.
2. From the displayed WordArt gallery, select the WordArt style you want to apply.
3. On the **Format** contextual tab, in the **WordArt Styles** group, select an option.
   - Select the **Quick Styles** option to apply quick styles to text.
   - Select the **Text Fill** option to apply the text fill color.
   - Select the **Text Outline** option to apply the outline to text.
   - Select the **Text Effects** option to apply various text effects.

ACTIVITY 2-2
Applying Quick Styles to a Document

Data Files:

C:\084574Data\Modifying Documents\OGC Overview.docx

Before You Begin:
The Word application is open.

Scenario:
You need to create a document and send it to some of your company's new clients. Your manager has approved the content, but has asked you to ensure that the company's name is displayed in a distinct style throughout the document.

---

1. Format the text "OGC Properties."

   a. Navigate to the C:\084574Data\Modifying Documents folder and open the OGC Overview.docx file.

   b. Close the **Navigation** pane.

   c. In the paragraph below the heading "About Us," in the first line, click before the text "OGC," hold down **Shift,** and click after the text "Properties."

   d. On the Mini toolbar, click the **Bold** button.

   e. On the Mini toolbar, from the **Font Color** gallery, in the **Standard Colors** section, select the **Dark Red** color.

   f. On the Mini toolbar, from the **Font Size** drop-down list, select **14.**

---

2. Save the applied format as a quick style.

   a. On the **Home** tab, in the **Styles** group, click the **More** button, and from the displayed gallery, select **Save Selection as a New Quick Style.**

   b. In the **Create New Style from Formatting** dialog box, in the **Name** text box, type *ogc_prop* and click **OK.**

   c. On the **Home** tab, in the **Styles** group, click the **More** button.

d. Observe that the **ogc_prop** style is added to the **Styles** gallery.

e. Click away from the **Styles** gallery to close it.

3. Apply the **ogc_prop** quick style to all other occurrences of the text "OGC Properties."

a. In the second paragraph, in the first line, click before the text "OGC," hold down **Shift,** and click after the text "Properties."

b. On the **Home** tab, in the **Styles** group, click the **More** button, and from the displayed gallery, select the **ogc_prop** style.

c. Observe that the custom quick style is applied to the text.

> *Description of Our Firm*
>
> OGC Properties offers a functional delivery service around a true single point of contact, with a team of experienced, diverse professionals. Our point of difference from other firms may be that our caseloads are limited; when you need help, the person you

d. Similarly, apply the **ogc_prop** quick style to all the other occurrences of the text "OGC Properties" in the document.

4. Save the document.

a. Select the **File** tab and choose **Save As.**

b. In the **Save As** dialog box, in the **File name** text box, type *My OGC Overview.docx* and click **Save.**

ACTIVITY 2-3
Modifying an Existing Style

Before You Begin:

The My OGC Overview.docx document is open.

Scenario:

You have highlighted your company's name with a distinct and consistent look. Having explored and implemented the Quick Style feature, you find that one Quick Style option, which you use frequently, comes in handy except that you need to make a couple of changes to it to suit your needs. You want to modify the existing style so that you can use it in the future.

1. Modify the attributes of the **ogc_prop** style.

   a. On the **Home** tab, in the **Styles** group, right-click the **ogc_prop** style and choose **Modify.**

   b. In the **Modify Style** dialog box, in the **Formatting** section, from the Font drop-down list, select **Arial.**

   c. From the Font Size drop-down list, select **12.**

   d. From the **Font Color** gallery, in the **Standard Colors** section, select the eighth option to apply the **Blue** color and click **OK.**

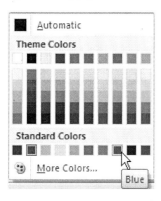

2. Save the modified style set and then save and close the document.

   a. On the **Home** tab, in the **Styles** group, from the **Change Styles** drop-down list, select **Style Set,** and from the displayed list, select **Save as Quick Style Set.**

   b. In the **Save Quick Style Set** dialog box, in the **File name** text box, type *My OGC Style*

   c. Observe that the quick style set is saved in the **Word Templates (*.dotx)** format.

   d. Click **Save** to save the quick style set.

   e. In the **Styles** group, from the **Change Styles** drop-down list, select **Style Set.**

f. Observe that the new style set, **My OGC Style,** is added to the **Style Set** drop-down list and click anywhere outside the list to close it.

g. Save and close the file.

TOPIC C
Add SmartArt Graphics

You applied text styles to enhance the visual appeal of text in a document. In a similar way, some content is conveyed more effectively by using appropriate visual elements to lend a professional look. In this topic, you will add SmartArt graphics to a document.

Readers are increasingly bombarded with information from magazines, newspapers, websites, and other sources. With a variety of media vying for a target group's attention, you want to make every effort to ensure that important points in your content stands out. With Office 2010, you can break the monotony found in pages of text by presenting them using supporting graphics, charts, and shapes.

SmartArt Graphics

SmartArt graphics are layouts used to show the time line, developmental progression, or sequential steps in a process or workflow. The **Choose a SmartArt Graphic** dialog box provides options to insert SmartArt in a document. You can select a layout from the gallery of existing layouts, where they are classified into categories such as **List, Process, Cycle, Hierarchy, Relationship, Matrix,** and **Pyramid.** You can also incorporate additional design and formatting changes into these layouts by using the commands on the **SmartArt Tools** contextual tabs.

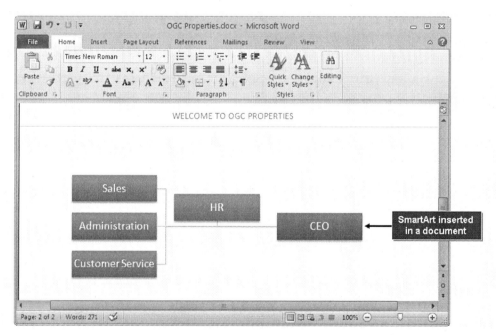

Figure 2-8: *The Choose a SmartArt Graphics dialog box displaying the different types of layouts.*

Categories of SmartArt Graphics

The layouts in the **Choose a SmartArt Graphic** dialog box are classified into nine categories.

SmartArt Category	Includes Graphics
All	That are a combination of all functional categories.
List	To display a list of items such as alternating hexagons and vertical box lists.
Process	To illustrate process flows such as step up process and continue process.
Cycle	To demonstrate process cycles such as a segmented cycle and pie.
Hierarchy	To represent hierarchical structures such as label and table hierarchy.
Relationship	To illustrate the relationship between entities.
Matrix	To display the relationship of four quadrants to a single entity.
Pyramid	To illustrate a hierarchical relationship.
Picture	To display a series of pictures with corresponding captions.

How to Add SmartArt Graphics

Procedure Reference: Insert a SmartArt Graphic

To insert a SmartArt graphic:

1. In a Word document, place the insertion point where you want to insert a SmartArt graphic.
2. On the **Insert** tab, in the **Illustrations** group, click **SmartArt.**
3. In the **Choose a SmartArt Graphic** dialog box, in the left pane, select a layout category.
4. In the center pane, select the desired layout.
5. In the right pane, preview the selected layout and click **OK** to insert the selected layout in the document.
6. Add text to the SmartArt graphic.
    - Click **[Text]** to enter text or;
    - Use the **Type Your Text Here** text pane to insert text.
        a. In the **Type Your Text Here** text pane, type the text.
        b. Press **Enter** to enter the text in the next shape.
        c. Close the **Type Your Text Here** text pane.

Procedure Reference: Apply Graphic and 3D Effects to SmartArt Graphics

To apply graphic and 3D effects to SmartArt graphics:

1. Select the desired SmartArt graphic.
2. If necessary, on the **Design** contextual tab, use the options to change the layout and style of the SmartArt graphic.
3. If necessary, click a shape in the SmartArt graphic, and in the **Create Graphic** group, from the **Add Shape** drop-down list, select the desired option to add another shape to the graphic layout.

4. Apply the desired style to modify the SmartArt graphic.

    ●   In the **SmartArt Styles** group, click the **Change Colors** drop-down arrow, and from the displayed gallery, select the desired color to apply to the graphic layout.

    ●   In the **SmartArt Styles** group, select the desired graphic style to apply to the graphic layout and click the **More** button to view additional graphic styles from the gallery.

5. In the SmartArt graphic, select a desired shape to apply shape and style effects.

6. On the **SmartArt Tools Format** contextual tab, in the **Shape Styles** group, select the desired option to apply the desired shape style and effects.

7. If necessary, add a bullet list within a shape.

    a. Select the desired shape.

    b. On the **SmartArt Design** contextual tab, in the **Create Graphic** group, click **Add Bullet.**

ACTIVITY 2-4

Creating an Organizational Chart Using SmartArt Graphics

Data Files:

C:\084574Data\Modifying Documents\OGC Structure.docx

Scenario:

Your company has recently hired several marketing executives at both the senior and junior levels. As the marketing manager, you need to create a document representing the organizational hierarchy and distribute it to the new employees as part of their orientation program. The organizational structure details are listed below.

1. First level - Marketing Manager – J. Rivera
2. Second level - Associate Managers – M. Muller and R. Moore
3. Third level - Marketing Executives – J. Dillon, R. Michael, and J. Jackson
4. J. Dillon and R. Michael report to M. Muller, while J. Jackson reports to R. Moore

---

1. Insert a SmartArt graphic.

    a.   Navigate to the C:\084574Data\Modifying Documents folder and open the OGC Structure.docx file.

    b.   Click at the end of the second paragraph and press **Enter** to move the insertion point to the next line.

> Moving the insertion point to the next line allows you to insert the SmartArt graphic properly without it realigning the content in a document.

    c.   Select the **Insert** tab, and in the **Illustrations** group, click **SmartArt.**

    d.   In the **Choose a SmartArt Graphic** dialog box, in the left pane, select **Hierarchy.**

    e.   In the center pane, select **Hierarchy,** which is the first SmartArt in the second row.

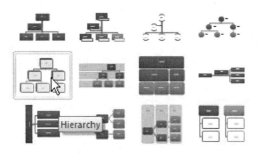

    f.   In the right pane, observe the preview of the selected SmartArt and click **OK.**

An enlarged preview of the Hierarchy graphic and information about the selected SmartArt can be viewed in the right pane.

2. Enter the organizational details.

   a. Close the **Type your text here** pane.

   b. At the top level, in the first box, click and type ***Marketing Manager*** and then press **Enter.**

   c. Type ***J. Rivera***

   d. Similarly, enter the associate managers' names and the marketing executives' names in the boxes provided at the appropriate levels based on the details provided in the scenario.

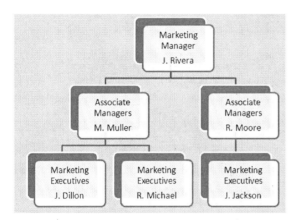

3. Format the SmartArt graphic and then save and close the document.

   a. Verify that the **Design** contextual tab is selected, and in the **SmartArt Styles** group, click **Change Colors.**

b. In the displayed gallery, scroll down, and in the **Accent 5** section, select the third option to apply **Gradient Range - Accent 5.**

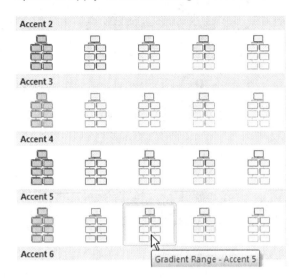

c. In the **SmartArt Styles** group, click the **More** button, and from the displayed gallery, in the **Best Match for Document** section, select **Moderate Effect,** which is the first style in the second row.

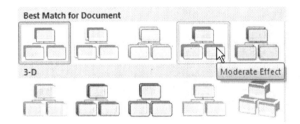

d. In the first box, click before the text "Marketing" and select the text till "J. Rivera."

e. Select the **Home** tab, and in the **Font** group, click the **Font Color** drop-down arrow.

f. From the **Font Color** gallery, in the **Theme Colors** section, select **Dark Blue, Text 2, Darker 25%,** which is the fourth color in the fifth row.

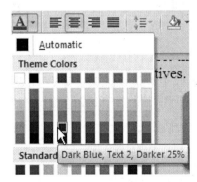

g. Click beside the diagram to select the entire organizational chart.

h. Select the **SmartArt Tools Format** contextual tab, and in the **Shape Styles** group, from the **Shape Fill** drop-down list, in the **Theme Colors** section, select **Aqua, Accent 5, Lighter 80%,** which is the ninth color in the second row.

i. Observe that the fill color of the organizational chart has changed.

j. Save the document as ***My OGC Structure.docx*** and close it.

TOPIC D

Insert Screenshots in a Document

You added SmartArt graphics to a document. In addition to this, you may want to insert images that provide visual reference that can add to your reader's comprehension. In this topic, you will insert screenshots in a document.

When working on documents, you may want to add images to supplement and enhance text in them, or you may need to quickly capture an image of an application window and insert it into a document. Office 2010 provides you with built-in tools to capture screens and modify images, without having to use any external software.

The Screenshot Tool

The *Screenshot* tool allows you to capture a screen of any window or a screen clip from your system and insert it into a document. This tool can be extremely useful when you are preparing a document about a software procedure or process that you may need to use as a reference and share it with other users.

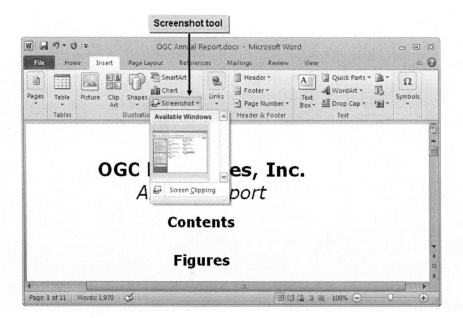

Figure 2-9: A screenshot captured using the Screenshot tool.

The Remove Background Tool

The **Remove Background** tool is used to remove backgrounds from images. Clicking the **Remove Background** button automatically selects the background of an image to give you an idea of the background area that you may want to remove. If the selected background area does not suit your requirements, then you can use the sizing handles to define the background area for removal.

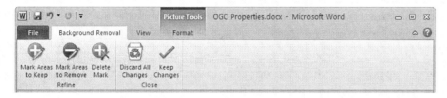

Figure 2-10: The Remove Background tool available on the Picture Tools contextual tab.

The Background Removal Tab

The **Background Removal** tab is displayed after you select a picture and click the **Remove Background** button in the **Adjust** group on the **Picture Tools Format** contextual tab. The **Background Removal** tab provides you with different options to define areas that need to be kept in an image and areas that need to be removed from it.

Crop and Compress Options

Word allows you to crop and compress images to scale them. The **Crop** drop-down list in the **Size** group on the **Format** contextual tab is used to crop images into various shapes, change aspect ratios, fill images, or resize images to fit them into a document. The **Compress** command in the **Adjust** group is used to compress images to reduce the size of a picture. However, compressing images to reduce file size may lead to loss of image quality.

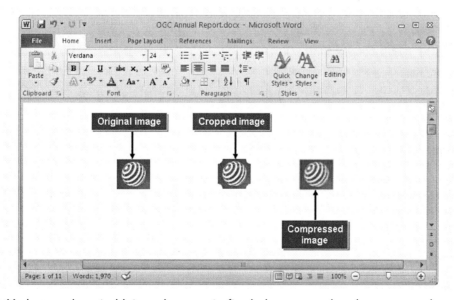

Figure 2-11: Images inserted into a document after being cropped and compressed.

How to Insert Screenshots in a Document

Procedure Reference: Capture Screenshots

To capture screenshots:

1. Place the insertion point at the desired location in a document.
2. Select the **Insert** tab.
3. Capture the screenshot.

   - In the **Illustrations** group, click **Screenshot,** and from the displayed gallery, select the window that you want to capture or;
   - In the **Illustrations** group, click **Screenshot,** and from the displayed gallery, select **Screen Clipping** and click and drag the marquee to mark the area of the window that you need to capture.

4. Verify that the screenshot is inserted into the Word document and if necessary, drag the image placeholder to reposition it.

Procedure Reference: Crop and Compress an Image

To crop and compress an image:

1. Select the image you want to crop and compress.
2. On the **Format** contextual tab, in the **Size** group, from the **Crop** drop-down list, select an option to crop the image.

   - Select **Crop** to crop the image.
   - Select **Crop to Shape** to crop the picture to any of the available shapes.
   - Select **Aspect Ratio** to crop the image to any of the ratios.
   - Select **Fill** to fill the remaining part of the picture.
   - Select **Fit** to fit the picture in the picture area.

3. On the **Format** tab, in the **Adjust** group, click the **Compress** button.
4. In the **Compress Pictures** dialog box, select an option to compress the image.

   - In the **Compression options** section, check the **Apply only to this picture** check box to compress only this image.
   - In the **Compression options** section, check the **Delete cropped areas of pictures** check box.
   - In the **Target output** section, select the available options to compress the image.

ACTIVITY 2-5
Capturing and Editing Screenshots

Data Files:

C:\084574Data\Modifying Documents\Cofee Makers.docx

Before You Begin:

1. Open Internet Explorer, and in the Address bar, type **www.everythingforcoffee.com** to launch the website.

2. If necessary, close the pop-up blocker.

3. The Word application is open.

Scenario:

In your document about the different types of coffee beans and coffee makers, you want to display a list of products available in your company. The product list is found on your company's website. You decide to capture an image of the product list details and add it to your document. Also, you decide to edit the image to suit your company's presentation standards.

---

1. Display the image to be captured.

    a. On the **Home** page, click the **Gourmet Beans** link.

    b. On the Gourmet Beans page, at the bottom-right corner, click the **Products List** link to display the products list in a separate pop-up window.

    c. Switch to the Word application window.

    d. Navigate to the C:\084574Data\Modifying Documents folder and open the Coffee Makers.docx file.

    e. Under the heading "Gourmet Beans", at the end of the third paragraph, place the insertion point and press **Enter**.

---

2. Capture a screenshot of the gourmet beans window.

    a. Select the **Insert** tab, and in the **Illustrations** group, click **Screenshot.**

    b. From the displayed gallery, in the **Available Windows** section, select the gourmet beans window to capture it.

    c. Observe that the image of the screenshot is inserted in the document and the **Picture Tools Format** contextual tab is displayed.

3. Edit the image.

    a. On the **Picture Tools Format** contextual tab, in the **Size** group, click the **Crop** button.

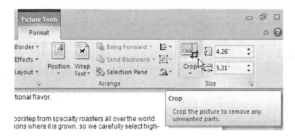

    b. Click and drag the top-center cropping handle downward until the border touches the gray line above the **Gourmet Beans** heading.

    c. Click and drag the bottom-center cropping handle upward until the border touches the gray line above the status bar.

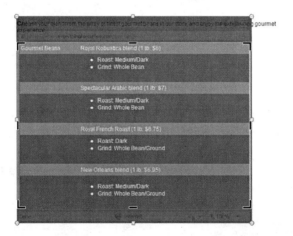

    d. Click outside the selection to view the edited picture.

    e. Select the image, and on the **Picture Tools Format** contextual tab, in the **Adjust** group, click the **Compress Pictures** button.

    f. In the **Compress Pictures** dialog box, click **OK.**

    g. Save the document as *My Coffee Makers.docx* and close it.

    h. Close the internet explorer windows.

TOPIC E
Compare Reviewed Documents

You created a document and added screenshots to increase the visual appeal and clarity of it. The document is now ready to be reviewed. As with many types of official documents sent to the client, the document might go through multiple rounds of review. Word 2010 allows for feedback from different sources to be consolidated and incorporated into documents with ease. In this topic, you will compare reviewed documents.

Sifting through multiple versions of the same document to hunt for suggested changes by reviewers can be a daunting task. In addition, you run the risk of missing crucial information and, ultimately, the integrity of your document can be threatened. With Word 2010, you can quickly and easily find all the changes that have been made to documents by using a few simple review commands.

The Compare Feature

The *Compare* feature enables you to combine or compare different versions of a document and check for information that may have been deleted, modified, moved, or replaced in the original document. This feature is available in the **Compare** group of the **Review** tab.

The Compare feature has two options that help you find all suggestions and review comments placed in a document, regardless of who has made them.

Option	Description
Compare	Displays what has changed between the two documents being compared. On selecting this option, Word displays four panes. The extreme left pane displays only the changes that are made. The pane in the center displays the compared document in which changes are tracked. The panes on the right display the original and revised documents.
Combine	Combines revisions from different authors into one single document. Selecting this option displays four panes. The extreme left pane displays only changes that are made. The pane in the center displays the combined document in which changes are tracked. The panes on the right display the original and revised documents.

The Tri-Pane Review Panel

The *Tri-Pane Review* panel is used to view and compare two different versions of a document along with the view that combines modifications from both versions. You can scroll simultaneously in all three views, making it easier to compare different versions of the same document. The **Tri-Pane Review** panel is displayed when you click the **Compare** command in the **Compare** group.

Figure 2-12: *The Review pane listing the changes and comments made by a reviewer.*

How to Compare Reviewed Documents

Procedure Reference: Compare Reviewed Documents

To compare reviewed documents:

1. Select the **Review** tab.

2. Compare the reviewed document with another document.

    - Compare two versions of a document.

        a. In the **Compare** group, from the **Compare** drop-down list, select **Compare.**

        b. In the **Compare Documents** dialog box, click the Browse button and open the original document.

        c. Click the Browse button, open the revised document, and click **OK.**

        d. In the **Microsoft Word** message box, click **Yes.**

    - Combining revisions from two authors.

        a. In the **Compare** group, from the **Compare** drop-down list, select **Combine.**

        b. In the **Combine Documents** dialog box, click the Browse button and open the original document.

        c. Click the Browse button and open the revised document.

        d. In the **Combine Documents** dialog box, click **OK.**

3. On the **Review** tab, in the **Changes** group, click the **Accept** button to accept the changes made in the reviewed document.

4. On the **Review** tab, in the **Changes** group, click the **Reject** button to reject the changes made in the reviewed document.

5. If necessary, click the **Previous** or **Next** button to move to the previous or the next edit in the compared document.

Procedure Reference: Change the Compare Options

To change the compare options:

1. Open a Word document.

2. Change the position of the **Reviewing** pane.

   a. Select the **Review** tab, and in the **Tracking** group, click **Reviewing Pane** to view the summary of changes at the side of the window.

   b. Click the **Reviewing Pane** drop-down arrow and select **Reviewing Pane Horizontal** to view the summary at the bottom of the window, or select **Reviewing Pane Vertical** to view the summary in the left side of the window.

3. If necessary, in the **Tracking** group, click **Show Markup,** then click **Reviewers,** and select only the reviewers whose changes you want to view.

4. Click **Previous** or **Next** to navigate and accept or reject the changes suggested by the reviewers.

   - From the **Accept** drop-down list, select the required option.

   - From the **Reject** drop-down list, select the required option.

5. Save and close the document.

ACTIVITY 2-6
Comparing the Changes Made to a Document

Data Files:

C:\084574Data\Modifying Documents\Management.docx, C:\084574Data\Modifying Documents\Management Reviewed.docx

Before You Begin:
The Word application is open.

Scenario:
You need to prepare a report about your management team and deliver it to a few prospective clients. You have worked on the report and sent it to your manager for review. You receive the document back with some changes tracked. Before accepting the changes, you want to compare the original and revised versions of the document.

---

1. Compare the original and revised documents.

   a. On the Ribbon, select the **Review** tab, and in the **Compare** group, click the **Compare** drop-down arrow, and select **Compare**.

   b. In the **Compare Documents** dialog box, in the **Original document** section, click the Browse button.

   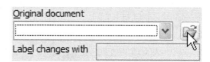

   c. Navigate to the C:\084574Data\Modifying Documents folder and open the Management.docx file.

   d. In the **Revised document** section, click the Browse button.

   e. Navigate to the C:\084574Data\Modifying Documents folder and open the Management Reviewed.docx file.

   f. In the **Compare Documents** dialog box, click **OK.**

   g. In the **Microsoft Word** message box, click **Yes.**

   h. Observe that the Reviewing pane is displayed on the left and the Tri-Pane Review pane on the right displays the compared, original, and revised documents.

---

2. Change the compare options and accept the changes in the document.

   a. On the **Review** tab, in the **Tracking** group, from the **Reviewing Pane** drop-down list, select **Reviewing Pane Horizontal.**

   b. Notice that the Reviewing pane appears at the bottom of the screen.

   c. In the **Tracking** group, click the **Track Changes** drop-down arrow and select **Change Tracking Options.**

d. In the **Track Changes Options** dialog box, in the **Markup** section, from the **Insertions** drop-down list, select **Double underline** and click **OK.**

e. Notice that the lines inserted by the reviewer are denoted using a double underline.

Relocation Services[SR1]

We tapped three of the Company's top managers to serve as regional presidents of our Relocation Services operations nationwide: Pat Markus, President, Central Region; Daniel Ortiz, President, Western Region; and Chris Johnson, President, Eastern Region.

f. In the compared document, verify that the insertion point is placed before the heading "Management Team."

g. On the **Review** tab, in the **Changes** group, click **Next** to highlight the next edit.

h. In the **Changes** group, click the **Accept** drop-down arrow, and from the list, select **Accept All Changes in Document** to accept all the tracked changes in the document.

3. Save and close the document.

a. Save the document as *My Management Team.docx* and close it.

b. Close the Word application.

Lesson 2 Follow-up

In this lesson, you modified documents using various features available in Word 2010. Document creation and modification is now easier because these features allow you to create professional-looking documents along with various value-add elements.

1. **What changes do you foresee in the process of creating a document using word 2010?**

2. **Which new features do you consider are the most useful in Word 2010? Why?**

3 Working with Spreadsheets Using Microsoft Excel 2010

Lesson Time: 45 minutes

Lesson Objectives:

In this lesson, you will present worksheet data using Microsoft Excel 2010.

You will:

- Work with tables.
- Apply a formula.
- Apply enhanced conditional formatting.
- Create charts.
- Create Sparklines.
- Work with PivotTables and PivotCharts.

Introduction

You have used some of the latest feature enhancements in Microsoft Word. The latest release of Office 2010 also has enhancements for improving the management, presentation, and distribution of worksheets. In this lesson, you will work with the new and enhanced features in Microsoft Excel 2010.

Depending on your role in an organization, you may have a need to manipulate large volumes of data within a short period of time. Another challenge with data is to present it, not only for those with an intimate knowledge of it, but also for those who may not be familiar with data sets, and yet need to comprehend and interpret data correctly. Excel 2010 offers visual enhancements that not only allow you to turn a worksheet filled with data into an interactive one, but also to facilitate the management of voluminous data.

TOPIC A

Work with Tables

You modified documents using Word 2010 to present data in a visually appealing format. You may now need to present numerical data effectively using Excel. In this topic, you will organize data in Excel using enhanced table formats.

Imagine you have to deal with large amounts of data that you need to process and analyze. Don't you think if the same data is segregated and arranged in a structured format would make the task easier? Excel provides you with various features and tools that help you process and analyze data.

Excel Table Enhancements

Using Excel, you can easily insert a table in a worksheet or select data from a cell range to be included in a table. You can also add headers to a table that appear as column headers when you scroll down a large table. You can associate row headers with their corresponding data using banded rows in a table. AutoFilters that appear by default in each table column allow you to filter data based on a specific parameter. Excel also allows you to sort data either alphabetically or based on cell color. You can also select preset tables from the Table Styles gallery.

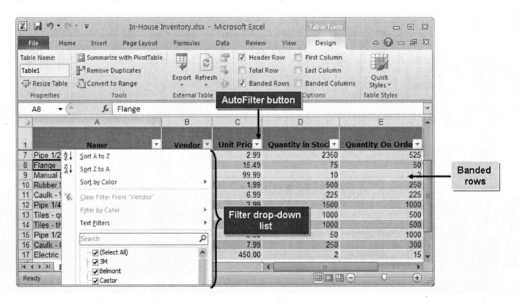

Figure 3-1: *A table displaying the enhancements to Excel.*

Excel Template Enhancements

Excel 2010 includes additional template categories with templates that you can use to create a variety of professional-looking spreadsheets. You can either use templates that are installed with Office 2010, or download additional templates from Microsoft Office Online. You can also customize templates to suit specific requirements.

How to Work with Tables

Procedure Reference: Convert Data into a Table

To convert data into a table:

1. Open an Excel worksheet and select the range of cells to be displayed as a table.
2. On the **Insert** tab, in the **Tables** group, click **Table.**
3. If necessary, in the **Create Table** dialog box, in the **Where is the data for your table** text box, modify the data range for the table.
4. If necessary, check the **My table has headers** check box to use the information in the first table row as header for the table.

 If you do not check the **My table has headers** check box in the **Create Table** dialog box, then the table will be displayed with the default header names.

5. Click **OK** to format the data as a table.

Procedure Reference: Convert a Table to a Data Range

To convert a table to a data range:

1. Open an Excel worksheet with a table and select the table.
2. On the **Table Tools** tool tab, on the **Design** contextual tab, in the **Tools** group, click **Convert to Range.**
3. In the **Microsoft Excel** message box, click **Yes** to convert the table to a normal range.

 When you convert a table into a normal range of cells, the **Table Tools** tool tab on the Ribbon disappears.

Procedure Reference: Filter Data in a Table

To filter data in a table:

1. In the table header, click the drop-down arrow to display the **AutoFilter** drop-down list.
2. In the **AutoFilter** drop-down list, in the **Search** text box, type the search item.
3. Check the check box of the item you want to filter.
4. If necessary, in the **Search** text box, type the next search item and check **Add current selection to filter** to add the new search item to the existing filter.

ACTIVITY 3-1
Working with Tables

Data Files:

C:\084574Data\Working with Spreadsheets\In-House Inventory.xlsx

Scenario:

You are using Excel 2010 to store data related to in-house inventory. You need to effectively present data and also discuss issues related to inventory levels at the weekly meeting. You plan to organize data so that the statistics can be clearly understood by all attendees.

---

1. Convert data into a table.

   a. Launch the Excel application.

   b. Navigate to the C:\084574Data\Working with Spreadsheets folder, and open the In-House Inventory.xlsx file.

   c. Select the cell range **A1:F17**.

   d. Select the **Insert** tab, and in the **Tables** group, click **Table.**

   e. In the **Create Table** dialog box, click **OK.**

   f. Observe that the selected range of cells is displayed as a table with column headers, filter drop-down arrows, and banded rows.

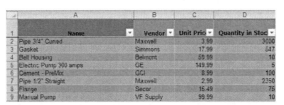

   g. Click any cell outside the table to deselect the table.

---

2. Use the table filter options to filter data related to rubber stops.

   a. In the Name header, click the Filter drop-down arrow. [▾]

   b. From the **AutoFilter** drop-down list, in the **Search** text box, click and type *ru*

   c. Observe that "Rubber Stop" is selected in the auto filter list and click **OK.**

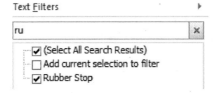

---

d.   Observe that only one row with the name "Rubber Stop" is displayed.

3.   Add another filter item.

a.   In the Name header, click the Filter drop-down arrow.

b.   From the **AutoFilter** drop-down list, in the **Search** text box, click and type *ti*

c.   Below the text box, observe that both the **Tiles** options are checked, then check the **Add current selection to filter** check box, and click **OK.**

d.   Observe that the table now displays the filtered items related to rubber stops and tiles.

Name	Vendor	Unit Price	Quantity in Stock	Quantity On Order	Quantity Backordered
Rubber Stop	VF Supply	1.99	500	250	0
Tiles - quarter-cut	Tile Place	4.99	1000	500	500
Tiles - third-cut	Tile Place	8.99	1000	500	500

e.   Save the file as *My In-House Inventory.xlsx.*

f.   Close the file.

TOPIC B
Apply a Formula

You formatted tables using enhanced Excel 2010 options to improve their layout and appearance. In the process of analyzing data, you may use calculated values in your worksheet. In this topic, you will apply formulas to perform calculations and identify the associated enhancements.

When you have data whose values are interdependent, you may need to perform numerous calculations to obtain the required information. It can be difficult to track errors in interdependent data, because their source information might be from different locations on the worksheet. The advancements in the use of formulas in Excel 2010 not only allow you to perform complex calculations easily, but also track and correct errors.

The Enhanced Formula Bar

The *Formula Bar,* located below the Ribbon, comprises the **Name Box,** the **Insert Function** button, and the **Formula Bar** text box. Enhancements to the Formula Bar include additional space to accommodate formulas within an option by expanding or collapsing the Formula Bar and choosing to hide it when not required.

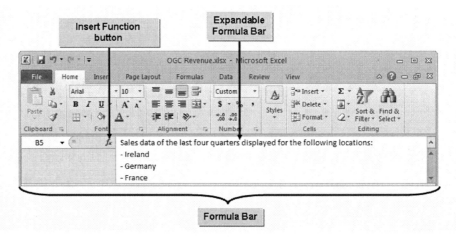

Figure 3-2: A sheet displaying the improved Formula Bar.

New Function Categories

There are two additions to the categories of functions: **Engineering** and **Cube.** These categories contain specialized functions for data operations related to engineering and cube.

The Formula AutoComplete Feature

The *Formula AutoComplete* feature simplifies the process of entering a function. When you type the equal sign followed by the first letter of a function, a drop-down list with all the available function names beginning with the same character is displayed. You can then select the required function from the list without having to remember lengthy function names or risk entering an incorrect function.

Formula Precedence and Dependence

The **Trace Precedents** and **Trace Dependents** options in the **Formula Auditing** group of the **Formulas** tab allow you to track a formula's precedence and dependence. When you track a formula, the precedence and dependence are represented as blue arrows. You can choose to remove these arrows using the options in the **Remove Arrows** drop-down list.

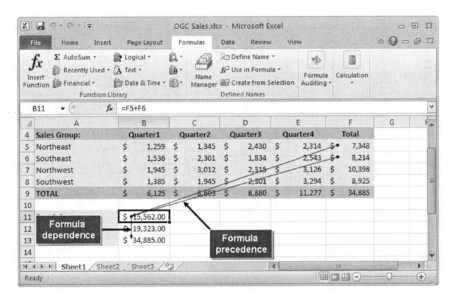

Figure 3-3: A worksheet displaying a formula precedence and dependence.

How to Apply a Formula

Procedure Reference: Apply a Formula Using the Formula Bar

To apply a formula using the Formula Bar:

1. Open an Excel worksheet with data.

2. Select the cell where you want to enter a formula.

3. Enter the formula.

    - In the Formula Bar, type the equal sign and the beginning letters of the function you need to use or;

    - In the worksheet, in the selected cell, type the equal sign and the beginning letters of the function you need to use.

4. From the **AutoComplete** drop-down list, select a function and double-click to insert the function.

5. In the **Formula Bar** text box, specify the appropriate values and arguments, close the parentheses, and press **Enter.**

6. If necessary, click the **Expand Formula Bar** or **Collapse Formula Bar** button to resize the Formula Bar to view the complete formula.

Procedure Reference: Name a Range of Cells

To name a range of cells:

1. Open the Excel worksheet with relevant data.

2. On the Ribbon, select the **Formulas** tab.

3. Specify a name for the range.

    a. Display the **New Name** dialog box.

    - On the **Formulas** tab, in the **Defined Names** group, click **Name Manager,** and in the **Name Manager** dialog box, click **New** or;

    - On the **Formulas** tab, in the **Defined Names** group, click **Define Name.**

    b. In the **New Name** dialog box, type the name, select the scope, specify the reference to cells, and click **OK.**

    c. If necessary, in the **Name Manager** dialog box, click **Close.**

Named Tables

A named table can be referenced within a formula. The name of the table should be specified in the **Table Name** text box available in the **Properties** group of the table **Table Tools Design** contextual tab before referencing.

Procedure Reference: Work with Formula Auditing Options

To work with formula auditing options:

1. Open an Excel worksheet with data.

2. Select the cells for which you want to audit the formula.

3. On the **Formulas** tab, in the **Formula Auditing** group, click the desired commands.

- Click **Trace Precedents.**
- Click **Trace Dependents.**
- Click **Remove Arrows,** or from the **Remove Arrows** drop-down list, select the desired option.
- Click the **Show Formulas** button.
- Click the **Error Checking** button, or from the **Error Checking** drop-down list, select the desired option.

 You can also hover the mouse pointer over the **Circular References** option and select an option from the displayed list.

- Click the **Evaluate Formula** button to display the **Evaluate Formula** dialog box.

Procedure Reference: Work with Calculation Options

To work with calculation options:

1. On the Ribbon, select the **Formulas** tab.
2. Select a calculation option.
   - On the **Formulas** tab, in the **Calculation** group, click **Calculation Options** and select an option.
     - Select **Automatic** to automatically recalculate interdependent formulas.
     - Select **Automatic Except for Data Tables** to automatically recalculate interdependent formulas, except for data tables.
     - Select **Manual** to enable the function to calculate values in the sheet before saving the workbook.

 The **Formulas** section of the **Excel Options** dialog box consists of calculation options. These options allow you to set either automatic or manual recalculation of formulas in a workbook before saving it.

- Click the **Calculate Now** button to recalculate all open worksheets.
- Click the **Calculate Sheet** button to recalculate values in the active sheet.

ACTIVITY 3-2
Working with Formulas

Data Files:

C:\084574Data\Working with Spreadsheets\OGC Sales.xlsx

Scenario:

You need to review the worksheet that your manager has planned to use in a presentation. You feel that the audience might not easily comprehend the data presented in the worksheet. You want to display the calculated values in the worksheet so that the audience can easily understand the data presented and draw proper conclusions. Also, you want to make sure that the correct data is used to calculate values.

---

1. Name a range as "Quarter1."

    a. Navigate to the C:\084574Data\Working with Spreadsheets folder and open the OGC Sales.xlsx file.

    b. Select the cell range **B5:B8.**

    c. On the Formula Bar, click the **Name Box,** type *Quarter1* and press **Enter.**

---

2. Create named ranges for Quarter2 through Quarter4 by using labels from the worksheet.

    a. Select the cell range **C4:E8.**

    b. Select the **Formulas** tab, and in the **Defined Names** group, click **Create from Selection.**

    c. In the **Create Names from Selection** dialog box, verify that the **Top row** check box is checked and click **OK.**

    d. From the **Name Box** drop-down list, select **Quarter1.**

e.   Observe that the data for the named range Quarter1 is selected.

Our Global Company
Sales Performance, Prior Fiscal Year

Sales Group:	Quarter1	Quarter2
Northeast	$ 1,259	$ 1,345
Southeast	$ 1,536	$ 2,301
Northwest	$ 1,945	$ 3,012
Southwest	$ 1,385	$ 1,945
TOTAL	$ 6,125	$ 8,603

f.   From the **Name Box** drop-down list, select **Quarter4.**

g.   Observe that the data for the named range Quarter4 is selected.

3.   Create named ranges for the Sales Group regions.

   a.   Select the cell range **A5:E8,** and on the **Formulas** tab, in the **Defined Names** group, click **Create from Selection.**

   b.   In the **Create Names from Selection** dialog box, verify that the **Left column** check box is checked and click **OK.**

   c.   From the **Name Box** drop-down list, select **Northeast.**

   d.   Observe that the data for the named range Northeast is selected.

4.   Use the **Name Manager** dialog box to rename the Sales groups.

   a.   On the **Formulas** tab, in the **Defined Names** group, click **Name Manager.**

   b.   In the **Name Manager** dialog box, verify that Northeast is selected and click **Edit.**

   c.   In the **Edit Name** dialog box, in the **Name** text box, type *NE* and click **OK.**

   d.   Similarly, rename Northwest, Southeast, and Southwest to NW, SE, and SW respectively.

   e.   Click **Close** to close the **Name Manager** dialog box.

   f.   In the **Name Box,** observe that the Northeast name range has changed to NE.

5.   Calculate the total sales for the East Coast and West Coast sales regions.

   a.   Select cell **B11.**

   b.   On the **Formulas** tab, in the **Function Library** group, click **AutoSum.**

   c.   In the **Defined Names** group, click **Use in Formula.**

   d.   Select **NE** and then type a comma.

   e.   From the **Use in Formula** drop-down list, select **SE** and press **Enter.**

   f.   Similarly, enter the formula in cell B12 to calculate West Coast sales.

g. Observe that the total sales is displayed for the East Coast and West Coast sales regions.

| East Coast Sales: | $ 15,562.00 |
| West Coast Sales: | $ 19,323.00 |

6. Check the source data of the formula.

   a. Select cell **B11,** and on the **Formulas** tab, in the **Formula Auditing** group, click **Trace Precedents.**

   b. Observe that the precedents are displayed with an arrow and the source data is marked inside the blue rectangle.

   c. Select cell **D6,** and on the **Formulas** tab, in the **Formula Auditing** group, click **Trace Dependents.**

   d. Observe that the dependents are displayed with an arrow and points to the data in cells that are dependent to the data in cell D6.

   e. Similarly, trace the precedents for cell B12.

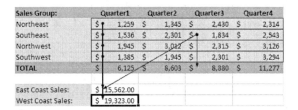

Sales Group:	Quarter1	Quarter2	Quarter3	Quarter4
Northeast	$ 1,259	$ 1,345	$ 2,430	$ 2,314
Southeast	$ 1,536	$ 2,301	$ 1,834	$ 2,543
Northwest	$ 1,945	$ 3,022	$ 2,315	$ 3,126
Southwest	$ 1,385	$ 1,945	$ 2,301	$ 3,294
TOTAL	$ 6,125	$ 8,603	$ 8,880	$ 11,277
East Coast Sales:	$ 15,562.00			
West Coast Sales:	$ 19,323.00			

   f. In the **Formula Auditing** group, click **Remove Arrows** to remove the arrows.

   g. Save the file as *My OGC Sales.xlsx.* and close it.

TOPIC C
Apply Enhanced Conditional Formatting

You applied formulas to perform calculations with data. In addition to performing calculations to analyze and interpret data, you may need to present data logically and in a visually appealing manner. In this topic, you will apply enhanced conditional formatting to data.

When looking at data, you often need to identify specific information in a data range. Examples include exceptions, unusual values, or variances that can be difficult to locate without special formatting. Excel 2010 provides advanced features that enable you to effectively and attractively present data by highlighting specific information.

Enhanced Conditional Formatting Options

The *Conditional Formatting* button in the **Styles** group on the **Home** tab enables you to format a data range by applying visual cues to cells to highlight key information. The **Conditional Formatting** options in Excel 2010 contain categories with predefined formatting options. Some of the conditional formatting categories contain galleries that complement the Live Preview feature, so you can preview a conditional format before applying it to the selected data.

Conditional Format Types

You can apply different conditional formats to cells using various format types in the **Styles** group on the **Home** tab.

Conditional Format Type	Used To
Highlight Cell Rules	Quickly find specific cells within a range of cells. You can format those cells based on a comparison operator.
Top/Bottom Rules	Find the highest and lowest values in a range of cells based on a cutoff value that you specify.
Data Bars	View the value of a cell relative to other cells. The length of the data bar represents the value in the cell. You can also customize the appearance of data bars as required.
Color Scales	Visually represent data distribution and variation. The shade of the color in this format represents higher, middle, or lower values. The color scale can be customized if required.
Icon Sets	Annotate and classify data into different categories. Each category is represented by an icon.

How to Apply Enhanced Conditional Formatting

Procedure Reference: Apply Conditional Formatting

To apply conditional formatting:

1. Open an Excel worksheet and select a range of cells or a table with numerical values.
2. On the **Home** tab, in the **Styles** group, click **Conditional Formatting.**
3. Apply the desired conditional formatting.
   a. In the displayed list, hover the mouse pointer over the desired conditional formatting type to display the respective gallery.
   b. From the gallery, select the desired conditional formatting option.
   c. If necessary, in the dialog box that is displayed, specify the conditions for formatting and click **OK.**

Procedure Reference: Manage a Formatting Rule

To manage a formatting rule:

1. Select the range of cells or the table to be formatted.
2. On the **Home** tab, in the **Styles** group, click **Conditional Formatting.**
3. From the displayed list, select **Manage Rules.**
4. In the **Conditional Formatting Rules Manager** dialog box, work with the options to manage a formatting rule.
   - From the **Show formatting rules for** drop-down list, select the desired option to specify the selection or sheet.
   - Click **New Rule** to create a formatting rule.
   - Select a rule, click **Edit Rule,** and in the **Edit Formatting Rule** dialog box, edit an existing rule.
   - If necessary, double-click a rule to display the **Edit Formatting Rule** dialog box and edit an existing rule.
   - Select a rule and click **Delete Rule** to delete an existing rule.
   - To the right of the **Delete Rule** button, click the **Move Up** or **Move Down** arrow button to move a rule up or down, respectively.
   - In the **Applies to** section, specify the range of cells for which formatting needs to be applied.
   - If necessary, uncheck the **Stop If True** check box for the corresponding rules.
5. Click **Apply** to apply the changes and then click **OK.**

ACTIVITY 3-3
Applying Conditional Formatting

Data Files:

C:\084574Data\Working with Spreadsheets\Product Sales.xlsx

Before You Begin:
The Excel application is open.

Scenario:
You have received the sales reports from various branches of your company for the previous year. You want to apply a format that will help you compare and highlight the sales trend across the branches in New York and Chicago. You also want to highlight the profit trend in the New York branch to help you make decisions on the sales strategy that you need to adopt in the future for that branch.

1. Preview the conditional formatting options.

   a. Navigate to the C:\084574Data\Working with Spreadsheets folder and open the Product Sales.xlsx file.

   b. On the New York worksheet, select the cell range **E2:E13.**

   c. Select the **Home** tab, and in the **Styles** group, click the **Conditional Formatting** drop-down arrow, and in the displayed list, hover the mouse pointer over the **Data Bars** option.

   d. From the gallery, in the **Gradient Fill** section, hover the mouse pointer over the first data bar at the top to preview the data bar conditional formatting applied over the selected range of cells.

   e. Hover the mouse pointer over the other data bars to view a live preview.

   f. Click **Conditional Formatting** again to close the drop-down list.

2. Apply a conditional formatting rule by referencing the Chicago worksheet.

   a. On the **Home** tab, in the **Styles** group, in the **Conditional Formatting** drop-down list, hover the mouse pointer over the **Highlight Cells Rules** option.

   b. From the **Highlight Cells Rules** gallery, select **Greater Than.**

   c. In the **Greater Than** dialog box, to the right of the **Format cells that are GREATER THAN** text box, click the **Collapse Dialog** button.

   d. Switch to the Chicago worksheet and click cell **E2.**

   e. In the **Greater Than** dialog box, in the text box, click after the letter "E" and press **Delete** to make the formula reference as a relative reference.

   f. Click the **Expand Dialog** button, and then click **OK.**

   g. Deselect the cell range to view the conditional formatting.

h. Observe that the shaded cells indicate that the direct expenses in New York were higher than that in Chicago.

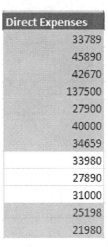

3. Apply a new rule to highlight the profit trend.

a. Select the cell range **D2:D13.**

b. On the **Home** tab, in the **Styles** group, in the **Conditional Formatting** drop-down list, hover the mouse pointer over **Icon Sets.**

c. From the **Icon Sets** gallery, in the **Directional** section, select the **3 Arrows (Colored)** icon set, which is the first icon set.

d. On the worksheet, click any cell to deselect the selected range of cells.

e. Observe that the green, red, and yellow directional arrows indicate the difference in profits.

f. Save the workbook as ***My Product Sales.xlsx*** and close it.

TOPIC D
Create Charts

You applied enhanced conditional formatting to make visual data analysis easier. You can also graphically represent data in visual formats for advanced analysis and interpretation. In this topic, you will create charts.

The monotony of reading through large amounts of data to interpret facts can cause fatigue, leading to loss of interest and attention. Presenting important points of the data using graphical representations facilitates comprehension and interpretation. Microsoft Excel 2010 provides enhanced options to represent data in various graphical formats to help with analysis.

Chart Enhancements

In Excel, charts are greatly enhanced with finer textures, better lighting effects, and more pre-defined styles and layouts that allow you to present data effectively. Tools to create charts are now readily accessible, and the process of creating a chart is also simplified. The chart formatting tools grouped under the **Design, Layout,** and **Format** contextual tabs allow you to access relevant formatting tools quickly, without having to navigate extensively. You can simply double-click a chart element to apply advanced formatting and use the displayed **Format** dialog box to set the desired formatting options.

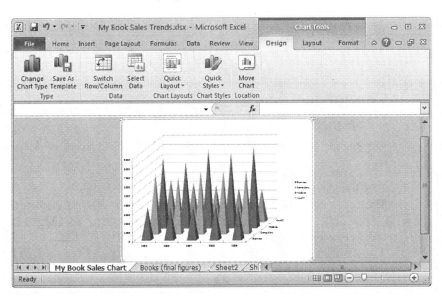

Figure 3-4: The Design contextual tab displaying the options for a bar chart.

Chart Data

In PowerPoint and Word, the chart data is stored in an Excel sheet. When you insert a chart in PowerPoint or Word, an Excel sheet with populated data based on the chart selection is launched. You can link a chart from an Excel workbook into your PowerPoint presentation or a Word document, enabling you to easily modify chart data and labels. When you edit the data in the spreadsheet, the chart on the PowerPoint slide or Word document gets automatically updated.

Enhanced Chart Tools

Chart tools are a group of contextual tabs that are displayed when a chart is selected. The commands on these tabs enable you to manipulate the appearance and layout of charts.

Contextual Tab	Description
Design	Provides options to modify the style, layout, data source, and type of a chart. The groups on the tab are: ● Type – Provides options to change the type of a chart and to save it as a template. ● Data – Provides options to switch between row and column data, as well as to edit the data source. ● Chart Layouts – Provides options to modify the layout of a chart. ● Chart Styles – Provides options to change the appearance of the chart to one of the preset styles in the **Quick Styles** gallery. ● Location – Provides options to move a chart to another worksheet or a new chart sheet.
Layout	Provides options for further customization of chart elements. The groups on the tab are: ● Current Selection – Provides options to format the selected chart element. ● Insert – Provides options to include shapes from the **Shapes** gallery or import pictures from a file. ● Labels – Provides options to manage labels on various locations of a chart. ● Axes – Provides options to manage the formatting of axes and gridlines. ● Background – Provides options to modify the background elements of a chart. ● Analysis – Provides options to add elements that aid analysis. ● Properties — Provides an option to specify a chart name.
Format	Provides options to format charts and chart elements. The groups on the tab are: ● Current Selection – Provides options to select and format a chart. ● Shape Styles – Provides options to modify the color, style, and effects applied to a shape. ● WordArt Styles – Provides options to preview WordArt styles and modify the fill color, line color, and effects. ● Arrange – Provides options to arrange, align, and rotate shapes, WordArt, or text boxes. ● Size – Provides options to modify the width and height of the selected graphical object.

Chart Templates

In Excel 2010, you can save charts that you created and formatted as templates so that you can use them in the future without having to design a chart all over again. You can access this feature by clicking the **Save As Template** button on the **Design** contextual tab. Charts that are saved as templates are automatically assigned the .crtx file name extension.

How to Create Charts

Procedure Reference: Create a Chart

To create a chart:

1. Open an Excel workbook with data and arrange the data according to the chart to be created.
2. Select the desired data and on the Ribbon, select the **Insert** tab.

 When you select a single cell with data, all the adjacent cells with data around the selected cell are automatically selected for chart creation.

3. In the **Charts** group, select the desired chart type.
   - Click a chart type to display the chart gallery and select a chart type from the gallery or;
   - Click the **Insert Chart** dialog box launcher to display the **Insert Chart** dialog box and select a chart type from the gallery and click **OK.**
4. With the chart selected, on the Ribbon, use the commands on the contextual tabs to format the chart.
   - On the **Design** contextual tab, use the options to change the chart type and chart layout, apply chart styles, and move a chart.
   - On the **Layout** contextual tab, use the options to modify chart properties and elements.
   - On the **Format** contextual tab, use the options to apply styles to the chart, arrange the chart as desired, or resize the chart.

Procedure Reference: Save a Chart as a Chart Template

To save a chart as a chart template:

1. In an Excel worksheet, select a chart.
2. On the **Design** contextual tab, in the **Type** group, click **Save As Template.**
3. In the **Save Chart Template** dialog box, in the **File name** text box, type a name for the template and click **Save.**

Procedure Reference: Create a Chart Based on a Chart Template

To create a chart based on a chart template:

1. Select the data for which you want to create a chart.
2. On the **Insert** tab, click the **Create Chart** dialog box launcher.
3. In the **Insert Chart** dialog box, in the left pane, select **Templates.**
4. In the right pane, select the desired chart template and click **OK.**

ACTIVITY 3-4
Creating a Chart

Data Files:

C:\084574Data\Working with Spreadsheets\Book Sales.xlsx

Before You Begin:
The Excel application is open.

Scenario:
You are doing a comparative analysis of the sales figures over the last five years in the Books department of your company. The information in your workbook does not provide a clear picture of the sales trend. So, you decide to present this data as a chart.

---

1. Create a chart.

    a. Navigate to the C:\084574Data\Working with Spreadsheets folder and open the Book Sales.xlsx file.

    b. In the Books (final figures) worksheet, select the cell range **A1:F5** to select the sales figures for the years 2006 through 2010.

    c. Select the **Insert** tab, and in the **Charts** group, click the **Bar** drop-down arrow.

    d. From the gallery, in the **Pyramid** section, select the first chart to create a **Clustered Horizontal Pyramid** chart.

    e. Observe that the selected data is presented as a chart and the **Design, Layout,** and **Format** contextual tabs are displayed on the Ribbon.

---

2. Modify the chart legend data and display the year on the vertical axis.

    a. On the **Design** contextual tab, in the **Data** group, click **Select Data.**

    b. In the **Select Data Source** dialog box, in the **Legend Entries (Series)** list box, verify that **Year** is selected and click **Remove.**

    c. In the **Horizontal (Category) Axis Labels** list box, click **Edit.**   [☑ Edit]

    d. On the worksheet, select the cell range **B1:F1.**

    e. Observe that the label range is populated in the **Axis Labels** dialog box and click **OK.**

f.   In the **Select Data Source** dialog box, click **OK.**

g.   Observe that the legend displays the book categories, and the years are represented on the vertical axis. The chart displays the sales generated in each book category for each of the last five years.

3.   Move the chart to a new chartsheet.

    a.   On the **Design** contextual tab, in the **Location** group, click **Move Chart.**

    b.   In the **Move Chart** dialog box, in the **New sheet** text box, double-click and type ***My Book Sales Chart*** and click **OK.**

    c.   Observe that the chart is displayed in a new chartsheet.

    d.   Save the workbook as ***My Book Sales.xlsx.***

ACTIVITY 3-5
Formatting a Chart

Before You Begin:
The My Book Sales.xlsx file is open.

Scenario:
Your worksheet discusses sales data, and you feel that the chart used in it is not suitable to project sales data. You want to make the chart appealing and add a title and then make this chart a standard chart format for your company.

---

1. Change the chart type.

    a. Verify that the My Book Sales Chart worksheet is selected.

    b. On the **Design** contextual tab, in the **Type** group, click **Change Chart Type.**

    c. In the **Change Chart Type** dialog box, in the left pane, select **Line.**

    d. In the right pane, in the **Line** section, verify that the fourth chart is selected and click **OK.**

---

2. Apply a chart style.

    a. In the **Chart Styles** group, click the **More** button.

    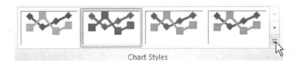
    Chart Styles

    b. From the gallery, select the **Style 18** chart style, which is the second style in the third row.

---

3. Enter the chart title.

    a. Select the **Layout** contextual tab, and in the **Labels** group, from the **Chart Title** drop-down list, select **Above Chart.**

    b. Observe that the **Chart Title** text box appears on top of the chart.

    c. In the **Chart Title** text box, select the text and type *Sales Data (2006 - 2010)*

    d. Triple-click to select the chart title text.

---

e. Select the **Format** contextual tab, and in the **WordArt Styles** group, select **Fill Tan, Text 2, Outline - Background 2** which is the first style.

4. Save the chart as a template.

   a. Select the **Design** contextual tab, and in the **Type** group, click **Save As Template.**

   b. In the **Save Chart Template** dialog box, in the **File name** text box, type *My Book Sales Chart* and click **Save.**

   c. On the **Design** contextual tab, in the **Type** group, click **Change Chart Type.**

   d. In the **Change Chart Type** dialog box, in the left pane, click **Templates.**

   e. Observe that the saved chart template is displayed in the right pane.

   f. Click **Cancel** to close the **Change Chart Type** dialog box.

   g. Select the **Books (final figures)** worksheet.

   h. Save the workbook.

TOPIC E

Create Sparklines

You worked with charts using enhanced chart tools. You may need to analyze large amounts of data graphically at a cursory level to identify trends. In this topic, you will create Sparklines.

Though you can have large amounts of data structured and organized within tables in a worksheet, graphically presenting the data can help you understand complex information, identify trends, and make decisions. In these situations, charts may not be an ideal solution because of the volume of data. Excel 2010 provides you with Sparklines that enable you to analyze data quickly.

Sparklines

Sparklines are miniature graphical representations of data in a worksheet. They are small, cell-sized charts that appear within the worksheet, and depict the numbers in the worksheet graphically. Sparklines are placed inside a cell, enabling you to compare data numerically and graphically, without having to create a complex chart for the whole data.

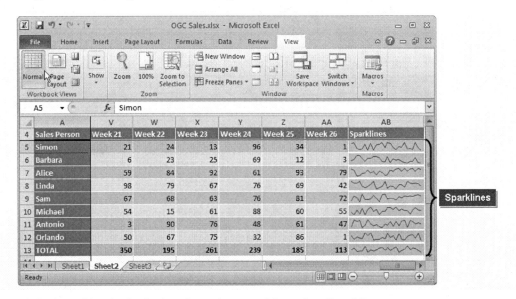

Figure 3-5: A workbook displaying the sales trend by using Sparklines.

Types of Sparklines

Excel 2010 allows you to create three types of Sparklines to represent data based on your requirements.

Sparkline Type	Description
Line	Data trends are displayed in the form of a straight or zigzag line.
Column	Data trends are displayed in the form of columns. Each data value is represented by a column whose size is proportional to the data value.

Sparkline Type	Description
Win\Loss	Data trends are displayed through the high points, the median point, and the low points.

Markers

Markers are used to highlight a point where the orientation of the trendline changes. Markers can be applied only to **Line** Sparklines.

How to Create Sparklines

Procedure Reference: Create Sparklines for Cell Data

To create a Sparkline for cell data:

1. Open an Excel workbook with data.

2. Select the cells that you want to use to create Sparklines.

3. On the **Insert** tab, select a Sparkline type.

4. In the **Create Sparklines** dialog box, in the **Data Range** text box, verify the range of cells you selected.

5. In the **Location Range** field, specify the cell on the worksheet where you want the Sparkline to appear and then click **OK.**

ACTIVITY 3-6
Presenting Data Using Sparklines

Before You Begin:

The My Book Sales.xlsx file is open.

Scenario:

The Books department in your company has given you the sales figures for each of its best selling book categories. You created a chart to display this information, but you are unable to view the sales trends by comparing their numbers. You decide to use the new features in Excel to present trend data in each cell.

1. Insert a Sparkline.

   a. Select the **Insert** tab, and in the **Sparklines** group, click **Line**.

   b. In the **Create Sparklines** dialog box, in the **Data Range** text box, select the cell range and type **B2:B5** and press **Tab**.

   c. Click cell **B6** to specify B6 as the location for the sparkline.

   d. Observe that in the **Create Sparklines** dialog box, in the **Location Range** text box, the location range is automatically populated and click **OK**.

   e. Observe that a line sparkline is created in cell B6.

A	B	C	D	E	F
Year	2006	2007	2008	2009	2010
Business	3500	3501	3654	3800	3647
Computer	6500	6157	6720	6800	6897
Hobbies	7582	7100	8500	8100	8752
Health	4568	4162	3920	3600	3459

2. Add Sparklines for the data displayed in other years.

   a. Autofill C6:F6 with the content in cell B6.

   b. Observe that the sparklines are applied for the other years.

A	B	C	D	E	F
Year	2006	2007	2008	2009	2010
Business	3500	3501	3654	3800	3647
Computer	6500	6157	6720	6800	6897
Hobbies	7582	7100	8500	8100	8752
Health	4568	4162	3920	3600	3459

   c. Save the workbook and close it.

TOPIC F
Work with PivotTables and PivotCharts

You created Sparklines for improving the comprehension and analysis of large amounts data. To selectively analyze data that is presented, you need to manually select the information and parameters for the analysis. In this topic, you will create PivotTables and PivotCharts for performing advanced analysis of data.

When you have large amounts of data to analyze, it may not be easy to perform advanced levels of analysis manually. Excel 2010 provides enhanced PivotChart and PivotTable features that enable you to focus only on the required data sets and analyze data.

Enhanced PivotTables

The *PivotTable* button in the **Tables** group on the **Insert** tab allows you to conveniently insert a PivotTable for selected data. PivotTables in Excel 2010 are more dynamic and efficient with the enhancement of the **PivotTable Field List** pane. The list now includes drop zones that allow you to not only drag fields into each of them, but also reorient and rearrange data and calculated values in multiple formats, enabling you to perform quicker analysis of data.

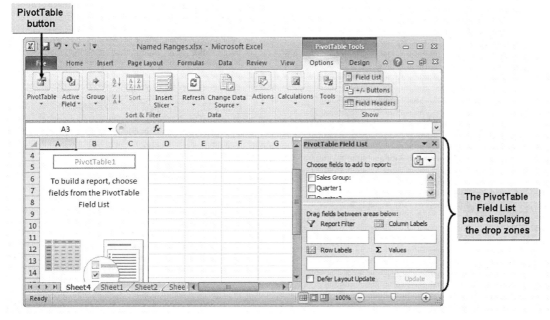

Figure 3-6: The PivotTable Field List pane displaying the drop zones to drag fields to various locations.

PowerPivot

PowerPivot is an Excel 2010 add-in that allows you to import data from various sources and analyze them using PivotTables. It is used for importing data from applications other than Excel and for processing such data using Excel tools. Using PowerPivot, you can integrate data from multiple sources and manipulate large sets of data with ease.

Calculations in PivotTables

Excel 2010 also includes the **Show Values As** context menu that displays calculations, which can be applied to fields in a PivotTable. There are six new calculation options in Excel 2010, including **% of Parent Row Total, % of Parent Column Total, % of Parent Total, % Running Total In, Rank Smallest to Largest,** and **Rank Largest to Smallest.**

Enhanced PivotCharts

You can access the *PivotChart* options from the **PivotTable** drop-down list of the **Tables** group. When you create a PivotChart, a PivotTable is automatically created. In Excel 2010, the right-click context menu allows you to change the position of fields on a PivotChart. You can also filter the data you want to view on the chart by using the drop-down lists displayed on the PivotChart and remove them by clicking the **Show/Hide Field** button on the **Analyze** tab. Once you manipulate the fields of the PivotTable, you can view the dynamic output on the PivotChart.

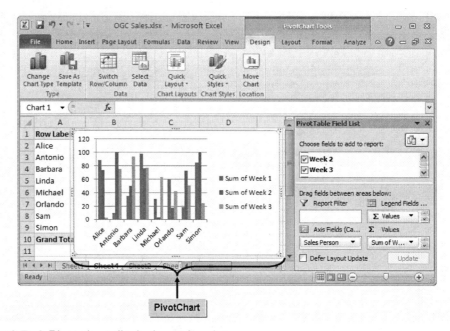

Figure 3-7: A Pivot chart displaying sales data.

Slicers

The *Slicers* feature enables you to slice data and include only the elements that you want in PivotTables and PivotCharts. It allows you to add and remove elements from the table display so that you can compare and evaluate data from different perspectives. You can also use Slicers with multiple PivotTables and PivotCharts to showcase data consistently in a variety of scenarios.

How to Work with PivotTables and PivotCharts

Procedure Reference: Create a PivotTable

To create a PivotTable:

1. Open an Excel workbook and select the data to create a PivotTable.
2. On the **Insert** tab, in the **Tables** group, click **PivotTable.**
3. In the **Create PivotTable** dialog box, specify the data range and the location for the PivotTable and click **OK.**
4. In the **PivotTable Field List** pane, specify the appropriate settings.
    *   In the **Choose fields to add to report** section, check the desired check boxes to be displayed in the PivotTable.
    *   If necessary, hover the mouse pointer over the desired field name and click the displayed arrow to sort and filter data.
    *   In the **Drag fields between areas below** section, drag the desired fields to the desired boxes.
    *   If necessary, check the **Defer Layout Update** check box.
5. Close the **PivotTable Field List** pane.

Procedure Reference: Format a PivotTable

To format a PivotTable:

1. In a worksheet, select a PivotTable.
2. On the Ribbon, select the **PivotTable Tools** tool tab to format the PivotTable.
    *   Select the **Options** contextual tab to format the options in the PivotTable.
    *   Select the **Design** contextual tab to design the layout and apply **PivotTable Styles** to the PivotTable.

Procedure Reference: Customize the Calculations in a PivotTable

To customize the calculations in a PivotTable:

1. If necessary, display the **PivotTable Field List** pane.
    a. Select the PivotTable report.
    b. If the **PivotTable Field List** pane does not appear, on the **PivotTable Tools Options** contextual tab, in the **Show/Hide** group, click the **Field List** button.
2. Display the **Value Field Settings** dialog box.
    *   In the **PivotTable Field List** pane, in the **Values** list box, click either the drop-down arrow or the desired field and choose **Value Field Settings** or;
    *   In the worksheet, in the PivotTable report, right-click a cell that is related to the values in the **PivotTable Field List** pane and choose **Value Field Settings.**
3. Customize the calculations using the **Value Field Settings** dialog box.
    a. If necessary, in the **Custom Name** text box, type the desired name to name the column.
    b. On the **Summarize By** tab, in the list box, select the desired calculations.
    c. Click **Number Format,** select a format, and click **OK** to format the field.
4. Click **OK** to customize the calculation of the column.
5. If necessary, repeat steps 2, 3, and 4 to customize the calculation of other columns.

Procedure Reference: Create a PivotChart

To create a PivotChart:

1. Open an Excel workbook and select the required data for the PivotChart.
2. On the **Insert** tab, in the **Tables** group, from the **PivotTable** drop-down list, select **PivotChart.**
3. In the **Create PivotTable with PivotChart** dialog box, specify the data range and the location for the PivotChart and PivotTable and then click **OK.**
4. In the **PivotTable Field List** pane, specify the appropriate settings.
5. If necessary, in the PivotTable, click the **All, Column Labels,** and **Row Labels** filter drop-down arrows, and from the displayed drop-down list, choose the desired filter option.

Procedure Reference: Format a PivotChart

To format a PivotChart:

1. In a worksheet, select a PivotChart.
2. On the Ribbon, select the desired **PivotChart Tools** tool tab to format the PivotChart.
3. On the selected contextual tab, in the desired group, select the appropriate command to format the PivotChart.

Procedure Reference: Insert a Slicer

To insert a Slicer:

1. Open a workbook with a PivotTable.
2. Select the PivotTable, and in the **PivotTable Field List** pane, select an item.
3. On the **Insert** tab, in the **Filter** section, click **Slicer.**
4. In the **Insert Slicers** dialog box, select an item and click **OK.**
5. In the Slicer that appears, click each item to observe the change in the corresponding PivotTable item in the worksheet.

ACTIVITY 3-7
Presenting Data Using a PivotTable and PivotChart

Data Files:

C:\084574Data\Working with Spreadsheets\Journal Sales.xlsx

Before You Begin:

The Excel application is open.

Scenario:

You are analyzing the sales revenue of your company's journals for the years 2008 to 2010. You want to create a report that will help your manager navigate the data randomly using different criteria such as sales figures for a year or a month in a year. Your manager also needs the data represented in a graphical format.

1. Create a PivotChart along with a PivotTable.

    a. Navigate to the C:\084574Data\Working with Spreadsheets folder and open the Journal Sales.xlsx file.

    b. On the Journal Sales worksheet, click cell **A4.**

    c. Select the **Insert** tab, and in the **Tables** group, from the **PivotTable** drop-down list, select **PivotChart.**

    d. In the **Create PivotTable with PivotChart** dialog box, click **OK.**

    e. In the **PivotTable Field List** pane, in the **Choose fields to add to report** section, click and drag the **Year** field to the **Legend Fields (Series)** box in the **Drag fields between areas below** section to display the legend in the PivotChart area.

    f. Drag the **Month** field to the **Axis Fields (Categories)** box to display the **Month** in the X-axis of the PivotChart.

    g. Drag the **Copies** field to the **Values** box to display the **Sum of Copies** in the Y-axis of the PivotChart.

h. Drag the **Income** field to the **Report Filter** box.

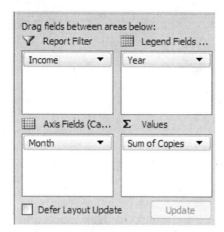

i. Observe that the PivotChart and PivotTable are created.

j. Close the **PivotTable Field List** pane.

k. Move the PivotChart to the right so that the last column in the PivotTable is visible.

2. Filter the PivotTable data.

a. In the worksheet, on the table, click the **Row Labels** filter drop-down arrow.

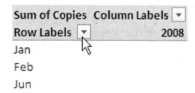

b. In the drop-down list, uncheck the **Select All** check box.

c. Check the **Jan** and **Feb** check boxes and click **OK.**

d. Click the **Column Labels** filter drop-down arrow.

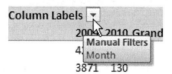

e. In the drop-down list, uncheck the **Select All** check box.

f. Check the **2010** check box and click **OK.**

g. Observe that the PivotTable and PivotChart reflects the total sales figures for the months of January and February in 2010.

3. Format the PivotChart.

a. On the worksheet, click the chart area to select the PivotChart.

b. Observe that the **PivotChart Tools** contextual tabs appear on the Ribbon.

c. Select the **Design** contextual tab, and in the **Type** group, click **Change Chart Type.**

d. In the **Change Chart Type** dialog box, in the right pane, in the **Column** section, in the second row, select the second chart type to select the **Stacked Cylinder** chart and click **OK.**

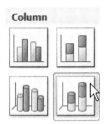

e. In the **Chart Styles** group, click the **More** button, and from the gallery, select the **Style 21** option, which is the fifth chart style in the third row.

f. Observe that the chart appears with the applied chart style.

---

4. Format the PivotTable.

a. In the worksheet, click a cell in the PivotTable to activate the **PivotTable Tools** contextual tabs.

b. Select the **Design** contextual tab, and in the **PivotTable Styles** group, click the **More** button.

c. In the displayed gallery, scroll down, and in the **Dark** section, select **Pivot Style Dark 6,** which is the sixth option in the first row.

d. Observe that the PivotTable style is applied to the PivotTable.

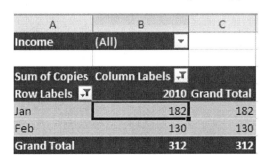

	A	B	C
Income	(All)		
Sum of Copies	Column Labels		
Row Labels		2010	Grand Total
Jan		182	182
Feb		130	130
Grand Total		312	312

---

5. Insert a Slicer in the PivotTable.

    a. In the worksheet, on the table, click the **Row Labels** filter, and in the displayed list, check the **Select All** check box and click **OK.**

    b. Click the **Column Labels** filter, and in the displayed list, check the **Select All** check box and click **OK.**

    c. Select the **Insert** tab, and in the **Filter** group, click **Slicer.**

    d. In the **Insert Slicers** dialog box, check the **Product** check box and click **OK.**

    e. In the **Product** Slicer, select each product to verify that the product numbers in the PivotTable changes to the corresponding product names.

    f. Observe that the sum of income in the PivotTable changes to the corresponding income on that product and save the workbook as ***My Journal Sales.xlsx.*** and close it.

    g. Close the Microsoft Excel application.

Lesson 3 Follow-up

In this lesson, you worked with the new and enhanced features available in Microsoft Excel 2010. Using features such as conditional formatting, PivotTables, and PivotCharts enables you to improve the management, presentation, and collaboration of your worksheets.

1. **How do you think the enhanced features in Excel 2010 will improve the organization and presentation of data?**

2. **Do you expect to use conditional formatting options for your job role? Give reasons.**

4 | Creating Dynamic Presentations Using Microsoft PowerPoint 2010

Lesson Time: 45 minutes

Lesson Objectives:

In this lesson, you will create dynamic presentations using Microsoft PowerPoint 2010

You will:

- Apply themes.
- Apply picture effects.
- Apply animation and transition effects.
- Add videos.
- Divide a presentation into sections.

Introduction

You worked with Microsoft PowerPoint 2003 (or earlier) to create presentations. PowerPoint 2010, with its redesigned interface, enhanced features, and result-oriented authoring tools, improves the process of creating dynamic presentations. In this lesson, you will create dynamic presentations.

Just as you need to create a blueprint for a house before you begin to construct it, you must decide on the various factors, such as the layout, theme, and effects, that impact a presentation, before you actually develop a presentation. PowerPoint 2010 offers several options that help you create effective and engaging presentations.

TOPIC A
Apply Themes

You worked with earlier versions of Microsoft PowerPoint to create presentations. PowerPoint 2010 provides numerous options to create effective layouts that are complemented by suitable themes and backgrounds. In this topic, you will create and apply themes and backgrounds.

When faced with the task of creating complex presentations in a short time, you will find that experimenting with different styles, selecting a specific format or layout, and applying it to the presentation on a trial and error basis requires a lot of time and effort. Wouldn't it be nice if you have the option of seeing what an effect looks like on the presentation just by a click or a mouse over without really applying the effect? Office 2010 provides features that help you achieve just that.

Themes

Definition:

Themes are design templates that provide a consistent visual look and feel for presentations. They not only affect just the background color of a slide, but also the color of visual elements and text present on it. Themes enable you to create professional-looking presentations and can be applied in a single click. You can choose to apply a theme either to all the slides or only to selected slides in a presentation.

Example:

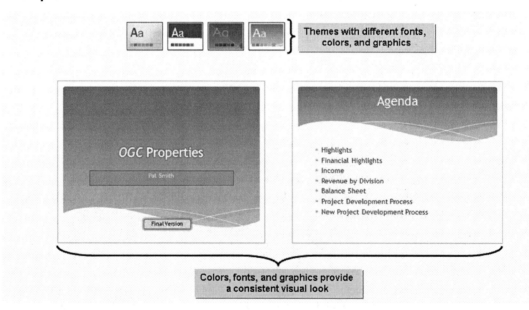

Figure 4-1: *Display of themes used on different pages to offer a consistent look.*

Theme Components

A theme encompasses three critical formatting components: **Theme Colors, Theme Fonts,** and **Theme Effects.**

Theme Component	Enables You To
Theme Colors	Apply a color theme to a presentation. You can also create, name, and save new theme colors to suit specific requirements.
Theme Fonts	Customize and modify the fonts used in a presentation theme. It consists of two different fonts: one for the heading and one for the body text.
Theme Effects	Change the visual effects in a built-in theme.

How to Apply Themes

Procedure Reference: Apply a Background Style

To apply a background style:

1. Open an existing PowerPoint presentation.
2. On the **Design** tab, in the **Background** group, click **Background Styles** and select the desired background style.
3. If necessary, check the **Hide Background Graphics** check box to hide any background graphics from being displayed on the slide.

Procedure Reference: Create a Custom Theme Color and Font

To create a custom theme color and font:

1. Open an existing PowerPoint presentation.
2. On the **Design** tab, in the **Themes** group, select the desired option.
   - Click **Colors,** and from the drop-down list, select **Create New Theme Colors.**
     a. In the **Create New Theme Colors** dialog box, in the **Theme colors** section, set the desired color options.
     b. If necessary, in the **Sample** section, preview the custom color theme.
     c. In the **Name** text box, type the desired name for the custom color theme.
     d. If necessary, click **Reset** to reset the color theme to the default theme.
     e. Click **Save.**
   - Click **Fonts,** and from the drop-down list, select **Create New Theme Fonts.**
     a. In the **Create New Theme Fonts** dialog box, from the **Heading font** drop-down list, select the desired heading font type.
     b. From the **Body font** drop-down list, select the desired body font type.
     c. If necessary, in the **Sample** section, preview the custom font theme.
     d. In the **Name** text box, type the desired name for the custom font theme and click **Save.**

Procedure Reference: Create a Custom Theme

To create a custom theme:

1. Open an existing PowerPoint presentation.

2. On the **Design** tab, in the **Themes** group, select the desired colors, fonts, effects, and background styles to create a custom theme.

3. Save the custom theme.

    a. In the **Themes** group, click the **More** button.

    b. Select **Save Current Theme.**

    c. In the **Save Current Theme** dialog box, in the **File name** text box, type the desired file name for the custom theme and click **Save.**

Procedure Reference: Format a Theme

To format a theme:

1. Open a PowerPoint presentation.

2. If necessary, on the **Design** tab, in the **Themes** group, click the **More** button, and from the displayed gallery, select **Browse For Themes** or **Enable Content Updates from Office.com.**

 You need to be connected to the Internet to use this option.

3. On the **Design** tab, in the **Themes** group, click the More button, and from the displayed gallery, in the **Built-In** section, select a theme to apply it.

4. In the **Themes** group, from the corresponding gallery, select a theme color, theme font, or theme effect that you want to apply.

5. If necessary, save the current theme.

    a. In the **Themes** group, display the **Themes** gallery.

    b. Select **Save Current Theme** to save the theme.

    c. In the **Save Current Theme** dialog box, in the **File name** text box, type a desired name and click **Save.**

ACTIVITY 4-1
Creating a Custom Theme

Data Files:

C:\084574Data\Creating Dynamic Presentations\Company Overview.pptx

Scenario:

Your colleague has asked you to review a PowerPoint presentation and make necessary changes before finalizing it. You find that the presentation is designed with different font types, font sizes, and color combinations, which may be distracting to the audience. You want to enhance the presentation so that the fonts and color schemes have a consistent and visually appealing look across all the slides.

---

1. Apply a prebuilt theme.

    a. Launch the Microsoft PowerPoint application.

    b. Navigate to the C:\084574Data\Creating Dynamic Presentations folder and open the Company Overview.pptx file.

    c. Select the **Design** tab, and in the **Themes** group, click the **More** button. ⬇

    d. In the displayed gallery, hover the mouse pointer over each theme to see a live preview of it.

    e. From the displayed gallery, in the **Built-In** section, select the **Median** theme, which is the seventh theme in the third row.

    f. Observe that the selected theme is applied to all the slides.

---

2. Create a custom color theme.

    a. In the **Themes** group, from the **Colors** drop-down list, select **Create New Theme Colors.**

    b.   In the **Create New Theme Colors** dialog box, click the **Text/Background - Dark 2** drop-down arrow, and from the displayed gallery, in the **Theme Colors** section, select the **Brown, Background 2, Darker 25%** color, which is the third color in the fifth row.

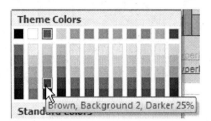

    c.   From the **Accent 1** drop-down list, in the **Theme Colors** section, in the sixth row, in the second column, select **White, Text 1, Darker 50%.**

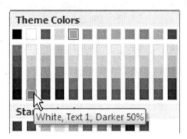

    d.   From the **Accent 2** drop-down list, in the **Theme Colors** section, in the first row, in the eighth column, select the **Gold Accent 4** color.

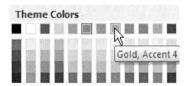

    e.   In the **Sample** section, observe that a preview of the color theme is displayed.

    f.   In the **Name** text box, triple-click the text "Custom 1," type *My Company Color Theme* and click **Save.**

    g.   Observe that the changes to the theme is reflected on all the slides.

3.   Define a custom theme font.

    a.   In the **Themes** group, from the **Fonts** drop-down list, select **Create New Theme Fonts.**

    b.   In the **Create New Theme Fonts** dialog box, in the **Heading font** drop-down list, scroll down and select **Verdana.**

    c.   In the **Body font** drop-down list, scroll up and select **Arial.**

    d.   In the **Sample** section, observe that a preview of the theme font is displayed.

    e.   In the **Name** text box, triple-click the text "Custom 1," type *My Company Font Theme* and click **Save.**

f. Observe that the change is visible on the current slide.

4. Save the custom theme.

    a. On the **Design** tab, in the **Themes** group, click the **More** button and select **Save Current Theme.**

    b. In the **Save Current Theme** dialog box, in the **File name** text box, type *My Office Theme* and click **Save.**

5. Check whether the newly added custom theme is displayed.

    a. In the **Themes** group, click the **More** button.

    b. In the displayed gallery, in the **Custom** section, hover the mouse pointer over the displayed theme and verify that the theme is the newly saved theme.

    c. Click away from the gallery to close the gallery.

    d. Save the presentation as *My Company Overview.pptx* and close it.

TOPIC B
Apply Picture Effects

You applied themes to enhance presentations. Illustrations, process diagrams, and pictures add emphasis and visual appeal to slides in a presentation. In this topic, you will work with graphical elements in a presentation.

A presentation is not just a series of slides with textual information. Flow charts, process related diagrams, and pictures have always been an integral part of slide shows. Enhancing the graphical objects on the slides helps you add a visual effect. PowerPoint 2010 has enhanced features that help you create complex diagrams and apply graphical effects to a presentation.

The Picture Tools Format Contextual Tab

The **Picture Tools Format** contextual tab includes commands to modify and enhance a picture. The **Adjust, Picture Styles, Arrange,** and **Size** groups enable you to adjust picture color and effects, add new picture styles, format picture layouts, and arrange and resize the pictures on a slide.

Group	Description
Adjust	Fine-tunes the color, brightness, and contrast of an object.
Picture Styles	Formats the overall appearance of a picture including the shape, outline, border, and special effects.
Arrange	Positions an object on a slide in relation to other objects or text.
Size	Resizes, rotates, or crops an object.

How to Apply Picture Effects

Procedure Reference: Modify a Picture

To modify a picture:

1. Open an existing presentation and select the picture to be modified.
2. If necessary, on the **Picture Tools** tool tab, select the **Format** contextual tab.
3. Apply the desired picture styles and effects.
    *   In the **Adjust** group, select the desired option to adjust the brightness, contrast, or recolor.
    *   In the **Picture Styles** group, select the desired picture style, shape, border, and effects.
    *   In the **Arrange** group, use the options to set the position of the image with respect to other objects on the slide.
    *   In the **Size** group, scale or crop the picture as desired.

Procedure Reference: Remove the Background from a Picture

To remove the background from a picture:

1. Open an existing presentation and select the picture from which you want to remove the background.
2. On the **Picture Tools Format** contextual tab, in the **Adjust** group, click **Remove Background.**
3. If necessary, in the Background Removal tab, in the **Refine** group, click **Mark Areas to Keep** or **Mark Areas to Remove** to modify the selected areas to be removed from the picture.
4. If necessary, in the Close group, click **Discard All Changes** to undo the changes.
5. Click outside the picture or click **Keep Changes** to remove the background.

Procedure Reference: Create a Photo Album

To create a photo album:

1. Open a blank presentation.
2. On the **Insert** tab, in the **Images** group, click the **Photo Album** button.
3. In the **Photo Album** dialog box, in the **Insert picture from** section, click **File/Disk.**
4. In the **Insert New Pictures** dialog box, navigate to the desired folder, select the desired image, and click **Insert.**
5. If necessary, in the **Insert New Pictures** dialog box, in the **Album Layout** section, from the **Picture Layout** drop-down list, select the desired layout option.
6. In the **Picture Options** section, check the **Captions below All pictures** check box.
7. Similarly, insert the rest of the pictures in the album.
8. If necessary, click **New Text Box** to add a text slide.
9. If necessary, rearrange the order of the pictures in the album.
    a. In the **Pictures in album** section, select the desired picture or text box.
    b. Rearrange the order.
       - Click the **Up** button to move the selected picture or text box up.
       - Click the **Down** button to move the selected picture or text box down.
       - Click **Remove** to remove the selected picture or text box from the photo album.
10. If necessary, in the **Album Layout** section, specify the options to modify the album layout.
    - From the **Picture layout** drop-down list, select a layout option.
    - From the **Frame shape** drop-down list, select a frame shape.
    - Select the desired theme.
       a. In the **Theme** section, click **Browse.**
       b. In the **Choose Theme** dialog box, navigate to the desired folder.
       c. Select a theme and click **Select.**
11. If necessary, in the **Picture Options** section, specify the picture options.
    - Check the **Captions below ALL pictures** check box to display a caption text below the picture.
    - Check the **ALL pictures black and white** check box to convert the picture into black and white.

12. If necessary, below the **Preview** section, set the desired options to adjust the image.

- Click the Rotate left button to rotate the image counterclockwise.
- Click the Rotate right button to rotate the image clockwise.
- Click the Increase contrast or Decrease contrast button to adjust the contrast.
- Click the Increase brightness or Decrease brightness button to adjust the brightness.

13. Click **Create** to create the photo album.

The PowerPoint Show (*.ppsx) Format

Saving a presentation in the .ppsx format allows you to view the presentation as a slide show, without having to open it in the PowerPoint application.

ACTIVITY 4-2
Applying Picture Styles and Effects

Data Files:

C:\084574Data\Creating Dynamic Presentations\OGC Properties.pptx

Before You Begin:

The PowerPoint application is open.

Scenario:

In one of the slides of the presentation that you are working on, you inserted a picture to complement content. However, you feel that you need to apply more effects and change the style so that the picture blends well with the slide layout.

---

1. Remove the background from a picture.

    a. Navigate to the C:\084574Data\Creating Dynamic Presentations folder and open the OGC Properties.pptx file.

    b. In the left pane, select slide 2.

    c. On the slide, select the picture.

    d. Select the **Picture Tools Format** contextual tab, and in the **Adjust** group, click **Remove Background.**

    e. Observe that portions of the picture are shaded in pink and that a background marquee is displayed on the picture.

    f. Drag the right, bottom, and left center sizing handles of the background marquee to the respective edges of the image.

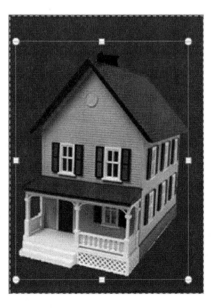

g. On the **Background Removal** tab, in the **Refine** group, click **Mark Areas to Remove.**

h. Click the chimney area of the house.

i. On the **Background Removal** tab, in the **Close** group, click **Keep Changes** to remove the background.

 You can also just click outside the selected picture to remove the background.

2. Apply a picture style.

a. In the **Picture Styles** group, click the **More** button.

b. From the Picture Styles gallery, select the **Beveled Matte, White** option, which is the second option in the first row.

3. Apply picture effects.

a. On the **Picture Tools Format** contextual tab, in the **Picture Styles** group, from the **Picture Effects** drop-down list, select **3-D Rotation.**

b.   From the displayed gallery, in the **Perspective** section, select the **Perspective Left** option, which is the second option in the first row.

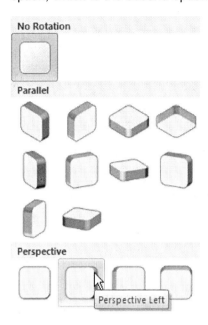

c.   Save the presentation as *My OGC Properties.pptx*

TOPIC C
Apply Animation and Transition Effects

You applied effects to pictures in a presentation. After enhancing pictures, you may want to increase the visual interest in the presentation by using animations. In this topic, you will apply an animation and transition effect.

When you present slides that contain only static objects and text, your audience may lose interest in the presentation. Animating the objects on a slide and adding special effects will help you capture and retain the attention of the audience.

Enhanced Animation Effects

PowerPoint 2010 allows you to add animations to objects by using the commands on the **Animations** tab. You can select an entrance, emphasis, exit, or motion path animation effect. You can also add more than one custom animation to an object. PowerPoint 2010 provides options to manage animations applied to slide objects, and includes the new **Trigger** command to set a trigger to start an animation. You can also apply variations to animation effects, set the start timing and duration, reorder animations, and preview animations using the **Animation Pane** options.

The Trigger Command

The **Trigger** command is used to start an animation when an event, such as clicking a shape, text placeholder, button, picture, or bookmark, occurs.

The Add Animations Gallery

You can also add variations to animations by using the effects in the **Add Animations** gallery. These effects are applied in addition to the existing animation effects.

The Animation Painter Command

The *Animation Painter* command provides you with an easy way to reuse animation effects. You can use the **Animation Painter** button to copy the existing animation of objects on a slide and apply it to other objects. You can also apply the desired animation effect to multiple objects that are not only within the same presentation, but also across presentations.

Figure 4-2: The Animation Painter command displayed in the Advanced Animation group.

The Animation Pane

The *Animation Pane* displays information about animations such as type, order, name, and duration of the effect applied to the elements on a slide. This pane also provides you with options to customize and preview the applied animation effects.

Option	Used To
The **Play/Stop** button	Preview the selected effect. When the preview is playing, the **Play** button toggles to **Stop.**
List	View the list of animation effects applied to the objects on a slide.
Advanced Timeline	Change the zoom levels on the timeline by using the **Seconds** drop-down list. It also shows you the start and end times when an animation effect occurs and enables you to navigate through the timeline.
The **Re-Order** buttons	Sequence the animation effects of the slide elements by moving an object up or down to make it play earlier or later.

Transitions

Transitions are special effects that appear while advancing slides in a slide show. A star appears under the slide number on the **Slides** tab in the left pane, to indicate that a transition effect is applied to that slide. You can change the transition speed and add sounds to slide transitions. You can also change or remove existing transitions applied to slides in a presentation. Transitions can be set to occur on a mouse click, key press, or automatically after a specified period of time during a slide show.

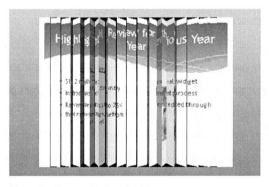

Figure 4-3: A transition effect in PowerPoint 2010.

How to Apply Animation and Transition Effects

Procedure Reference: Apply an Animation Effect to an Object

To apply an animation effect to an object:

1. Select the object that you want to animate.

2. On the **Animations** tab, in the **Animations** group, from the **More** drop-down list, select an animation.

3. If necessary, preview the animation that you have applied.

Procedure Reference: Animate Objects Using the Animation Painter Command

To animate objects using the **Animation Painter** command:

1. Select the object that has the animation effect you want to copy.

2. On the **Animations** tab, in the **Advanced Animation** group, double-click **Animation Painter** to copy the existing object's animation.

3. Click the object to which you want to apply the copied animation effect.

4. If necessary, apply the same animation to objects located in multiple places within the presentation.

5. Click outside the slide to deactivate the **Animation Painter.**

Procedure Reference: Change an Animation Effect

To change an animation effect:

1. Select an object or text.

2. On the **Animations** tab, in the **Advanced Animations** group, click **Animation Pane** to display the **Animation Pane.**

3. In the **Animation Pane,** select the animation that you want to change.

4. Change the animation as desired.

    ● On the **Animations** tab, in the **Animations** group, click the **More** drop-down arrow, and from the displayed gallery, select the new animation you want to apply.

    ● On the **Animations** tab, in the **Advanced Animations** group, click the **Add Animations** drop-down arrow, and from the displayed gallery, select the new animation you want to apply.

    ● On the **Animations** tab, in the **Timing** group, set the duration of animation.

5. If necessary, on the **Animations** tab, click **Preview** to preview the animation.

Procedure Reference: Apply Slide Transitions

To apply slide transitions:

1. Select the slides to which you want to apply a transition effect.

2. On the Ribbon, select the **Transitions** tab.

3. Apply the transition effect.

    ● In the **Transition to This Slide** group, select a transition or;

    ● In the **Transition to This Slide** group, click the **More** button, and from the displayed gallery of transitions, select a transition.

4. If necessary, in the **Timing** group, specify the desired options.

    ●   In the **Timing** group, click **Apply To All** to apply the transition effect to all the slides in the presentation.

    ●   In the **Timing** group, in the **Duration** spin box, select the duration for which the transition should occur.

    ●   In the **Timing** group, from the **Sound** drop-down list, select a sound to play along with the transition.

5. Select the **Slide Show** tab, and in the **Start Slide Show** group, select the desired option to view the slide transitions in a slide show.

    ●   Click **From Beginning** to start the slide show from the first slide.

    ●   Click **From Current Slide** to start the slide show from the current slide.

6. End the slide show.

ACTIVITY 4-3
Applying an Animation Effect

Before You Begin:
The My OGC Properties.pptx file is open.

Scenario:
While reviewing the presentation that you recently created, you observe that all the slides are static and not lively and interactive. You realize that by using a variety of ways such as by adding animation effects to introduce the content in the slides, you can draw the audience's attention. You decide to animate the first slide to begin the presentation on an interactive note.

1. Apply the **Float In** animation to the title placeholder.

   a. In the left pane, select slide 1.

   b. On the slide, click before the word "Our" to display the title placeholder.

   c. Select the **Animations** tab, and in the **Animation** group, click the **More** button and from the displayed gallery, in the **Entrance** section, select **Float In.**

2. Apply the **Random Bars** animation to the subtitle placeholder.

   a. On slide 1, click before the text "J. Rivera" to display the subtitle placeholder.

   b. On the **Animations** tab, in the **Animation** group, click the **More** button, and from the displayed gallery, select **More Entrance Effects.**

   c. In the **Change Entrance Effect** dialog box, scroll down and in the **Exciting** section, select **Whip** and then click **OK.**

3. Preview the animation effects applied to slide 1.

   a. On the **Animations** tab, in the **Preview** section, click **Preview.**

   b. Observe that the animation effects are applied to the objects on the slide.

4. Apply the subtitle's animation effect to slide 22.

   a. On slide 1, click before the text "J. Rivera" to display the subtitle text placeholder.

b. On the **Animations** tab, in the **Advanced Animation** section, click **Animation Painter.**

c. In the left pane, scroll down and select slide 22.

d. Scroll up and click before the text "Questions?" to apply the subtitle's animation effect to the slide.

---

5. Apply and preview a transition effect.

a. Select the **Transitions** tab, and in the **Transition to This Slide** group, from the gallery, select **Push** to apply the transition effect.

b. In the **Timing** group, click **Apply To All** to apply the transition effect to all the slides.

c. Select the **Slide Show** tab, and in the **Start Slide Show** group, click **From Beginning** to preview the transition effect as a slide show.

d. Click anywhere on the empty slide to display the animation that is applied to the title "Our Global Company."

e. Click anywhere on the slide to observe the animation that is applied to the subtitle "J.Rivera."

f. Click the slide to view the transition to slide 2.

g. Right-click the slide and choose **End Show** to end the slide show.

TOPIC D
Add Videos

You added animation and transition effects to a presentation. You may also want to include external content in the presentation that are relevant to the presentation's content. In this topic, you will add videos to a presentation.

The video capabilities of PowerPoint 2010 give you the advantage of not only adding videos to a presentation, but also effectively editing them without having to rely on any external applications or add-ins. The new video editing tools in PowerPoint 2010 allow you to control the quality and effectiveness of videos and create professional-looking presentations.

Video Tools Commands

The *Video Tools* tool tab comprises tabs with commands that enable you to edit, modify, and format videos. The video formatting commands are distributed within the **Format** and **Playback** contextual tabs. These contextual tabs provide you with various options to adjust the brightness and color tone, apply video styles and effects, arrange and resize videos, add or remove bookmarks, edit and trim videos, and apply playback options such as **Play Full Screen** and **Rewind after Playing.**

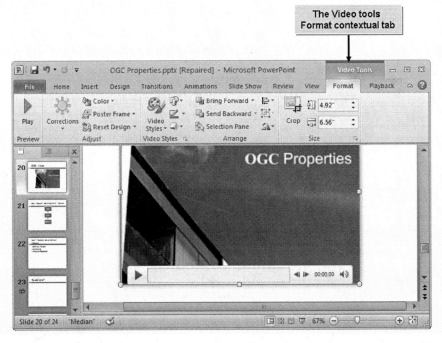

Figure 4-4: The Video Tools Format contextual tab displaying the commands used to format a video.

Video Styles and Effects

PowerPoint 2010 includes options to add styles and effects to the videos in a presentation. The **Video Styles** group on the **Format** contextual tab provides options to add subtle, moderate, or intense styles; modify the shape of videos; add borders and outlines using colors; and apply video effects such as **Shadow, Reflection,** and **Glow,** among others.

The Video Options Group

The **Video Options** group on the **Playback** contextual tab contains various components that you can use to set the playback options for a video.

Component	*Used To*
Volume	Set the volume of a video to a low, medium, or high level. You can also mute the video.
Start	Set a video to play automatically when switching to a slide, or on a mouse click.
Play Full Screen	Play a video on full screen during a presentation.
Hide While Not Playing	Hide the thumbnail that represents a video during a slide show.
Loop until Stopped	Play a video repeatedly until you stop it.
Rewind after Playing	Rewind a video to the first frame after it finishes playing.

How to Add Videos

Procedure Reference: Insert a Video

To insert a video:

1. Select the slide in which you want to insert a video.
2. Select the **Insert** tab, and in the **Media** group, click the **Video** drop-down arrow, and from the displayed list, select **Video from File.**
3. In the **Insert Video** dialog box, select a video file and click **Insert.**

Procedure Reference: Make Adjustments to a Video

To make adjustments to a video:

1. In a PowerPoint presentation, select the video to which you want to make adjustments.
2. On the **Video Tools** tool tab, on the **Format** contextual tab, set the desired options.
   - In the **Adjust** group, select the desired option to adjust the brightness and color settings.
   - In the **Video Styles** group, apply the desired video style and video effects.
   - In the **Size** group, adjust the size of the video to get the desired size.

Procedure Reference: Edit a Video

To edit a video:

1. In a PowerPoint presentation, select the desired video.

2. On the **Video Tools** tool tab, on the **Playback** contextual tab, in the **Editing** group, click **Trim Video.**

3. In the **Trim Video** dialog box, specify the start and end times to trim the video and click **OK.**

4. In the **Editing** group, specify the desired **Fade In** and **Fade out** time.

5. In the **Video Options** group, check the check boxes for the desired playback settings.

ACTIVITY 4-4
Adding Videos to a Presentation

Before You Begin:
The My OGC Properties.pptx file is open.

Scenario:
You need to highlight your company's activities using videos. You decide to use one of the company's promotional videos in the presentation, but you need to apply video styles and effects, and trim a section of the video so that it does not display a blank screen.

---

1. Insert a new video.

   a. In the left pane, scroll down and select slide 19.

   b. Select the **Home** tab, and in the **Slides** group, click **New Slide,** and from the displayed gallery, select **Title Only.**

   c. In the **Click to add title** placeholder, click and type *OGC Video*

   d. Select the **Insert** tab, and in the **Media** group, click **Video.**

   e. In the **Insert Video** dialog box, navigate to the C:\084574Data\Creating Dynamic Presentations folder.

   f. Select the **OGC Properties.avi** file and click **Insert.**

---

2. Apply styles and effects to video.

   a. On the **Video Tools Format** contextual tab, in the **Adjust** group, click the **Corrections** drop-down arrow.

b.   From the displayed gallery, in the **Brightness and Contrast** section, select the **Brightness: 0% (Normal) Contrast: +20%** option, which is the third option in the fourth row.

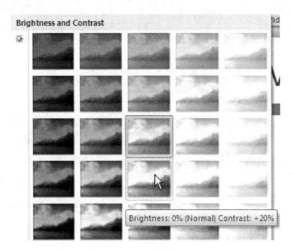

c.   In the **Video Styles** group, select the **Center Shadow Rectangle** video style, which is the second option from the left.

d.   In the **Video Styles** group, from the **Video Effects** drop-down list, select **Soft Edges,** and from the displayed gallery, select **2.5 Point.**

3.   Preview and trim the video.

a.   Select the **Video Tools Playback** contextual tab, and in the **Preview** section, click **Play.**

b.   Observe that the last few seconds of the video are blank.

c.   On the **Video Tools Playback** contextual tab, in the **Editing** group, click **Trim Video.**

d.   In the **Trim Video** dialog box, verify that the **Start Time** text box displays the start time as **00:00.**

e.   In the **End Time** text box, triple-click, type *00:08* and press **Tab** and then click **OK** to trim the video.

f.   On the **Video Tools Playback** contextual tab, in the **Preview** group, click **Play** to observe that the video is now trimmed to 8 seconds and the blank screen no longer appears.

g.   Save and close the presentation.

TOPIC E
Divide a Presentation into Sections

You added videos to a presentation. You may now want to apply further customizing options to slides so that you can quickly organize the slides in the presentation. In this topic, you will divide a presentation into sections.

Imagine a situation where you had to prepare a long presentation which included half a dozen subjects or more. All the slides in the presentation are displayed randomly, and you want to find a particular slide so that you can edit it. It would be a time-consuming effort if you had to rummage through all the slides to find the one you want to fix. This is particularly annoying when you do not have too much time at your disposal. PowerPoint 2010 gives you the advantage of grouping related slides into sections, so that you can quickly and easily identify the slides that you need to work on.

The Slide Section Feature

The *Slide Section* feature that can be accessed from the **Slides** group on the **Home** tab enables you to organize slides in a presentation. You can name sections in presentations to track groups of slides that belong to a category. Using this feature, you can add, rename, move, and remove a section. You can also drag slides from one section to another.

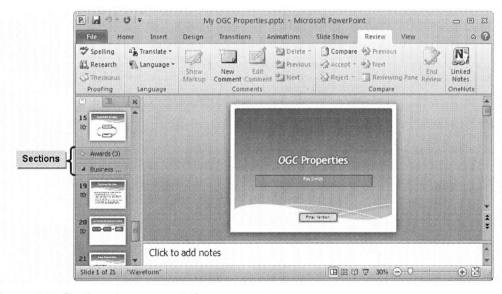

Figure 4-5: *Sections in a presentation.*

How to Divide a Presentation into Sections

Procedure Reference: Create a Section in an Existing Presentation

To create a section in an existing presentation:

1. Open an existing PowerPoint presentation.

2. Add a section.

   - On the **Home** tab, in the **Slides** group, from the **Section** drop-down list, select **Add Section** or;

   - Right-click between the two slides where you want to add a section and choose **Add Section.**

3. Rename the section.

   a. Display the **Rename Section** dialog box.

      - On the **Home** tab, in the **Slides** group, from the **Section** drop-down list, select **Rename Section** or;

      - Right-click the Section bar and choose **Rename Section.**

   b. In the **Rename Section** dialog box, in the **Section name** text box, type a section name and click **Rename.**

Procedure Reference: Rearrange the Sections in a Presentation

To rearrange the sections in a presentation:

1. Open a presentation with multiple sections.

2. Reorder a section.

   - Right-click a section title bar and choose **Move Section Down** to move the section to below another section.

   - Right-click a section title bar and choose **Move Section Up** to move the section to above another section.

 The **Move Section Up** and **Move Section Down** options are enabled only if there are sections above or below the current section.

ACTIVITY 4-5
Creating Sections in a Presentation

Data Files:

C:\084574Data\Creating Dynamic Presentations\OGC Properties Overview.pptx

Before You Begin:

The PowerPoint application is open.

Scenario:

You are preparing a presentation on your company's achievements. There are multiple slides in the presentation and your manager wants you to highlight the financial results of the company, followed by the performances of the company's meritorious staff. She wants you to organize slides in such a manner that the slides related to the financial aspects of the company can be easily distinguished from the slides that contain information about the performance of the employees.

---

1. Create sections to group the "Financial Overview" and "Awards" slides.

    a. Navigate to the C:\084574Data\Creating Dynamic Presentations folder and open the OGC Properties Overview.pptx file.

    b. In the left pane, scroll down and select slide 13.

    c. On the **Home** tab, in the **Slides** group, from the **Section** drop-down list, select **Add Section.**

d. In the left pane, on the **Slides** tab, observe that an **Untitled Section** title bar is displayed and that the slides below it are included in that section.

e. On the **Home** tab, in the **Slides** group, from the **Section** drop-down list, select **Rename Section.**

f. In the **Rename Section** dialog box, in the **Section name** text box, type *Financial Overview* and click **Rename.**

g. Observe that the section is named Financial Overview.

h. Select slide 10, right-click, and choose **Add Section.**

i. Right-click the **Untitled Section** title bar and choose **Rename Section.**

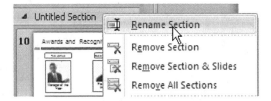

j. In the **Rename Section** dialog box, in the **Section name** text box, type *Awards* and click **Rename.**

2. Reorder the sections.

a. Right-click the **Awards** section title bar and choose **Move Section Down** to move the Awards section to below the Financial Overview section.

b. Observe that the sections, including the slides, are reordered.

c.   Select slide 19 and drag it below slide 22.

d.   Observe that the slide is included in the Awards section as slide 22.

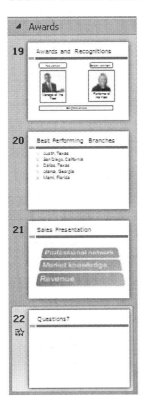

e.   Save the presentation as ***My OGC Properties Overview.pptx*** and close it.

f.   Close the PowerPoint application.

Lesson 4 Follow-up

In this lesson, you created effective and engaging presentations. This would enable you to present your content to a wider audience in a professional way.

1. **How do you think applying themes to a presentation will add value to it?**

2. **How do you think applying picture effects will enhance the effectiveness of a presentation?**

5 Working with Databases Using Microsoft Access 2010

Lesson Time: 1 hour(s), 15 minutes

Lesson Objectives:

In this lesson, you will work with databases using Microsoft Access 2010.

You will:

- Work with tables.
- Work with queries and macros.
- Create forms.
- Create reports.
- Work with external data.
- Design a database for the web.

Introduction

You worked with Microsoft Access 2003 to create and manage databases. You want to familiarize yourself with the additional features in the latest release of the software for improving the management, presentation, and distribution of your databases. In this lesson, you will be introduced to the new features available in Microsoft Access 2010.

For any work that involves managing a large amount of data, you need an application that helps you store, access, and link with the data of other applications. By using the new and enhanced features in Microsoft Access 2010, you will be able to create a robust and highly functional database that will help you manage large amounts of data efficiently, thereby increasing productivity.

TOPIC A
Work with Tables

You have used Access 2003 and other earlier versions to store and manage data. Although Access 2010, like all database applications, uses tables to store data, it provides certain features that enable you to easily manage, access, and modify data in a database. In this topic, you will work with tables.

Storing data in text files requires careful consideration of file size because the amount of data you can store in a text file is limited. Moreover, accessing and manipulating data in a text document can at times be cumbersome and may lead to errors or data loss. Databases enable you to store large and complex data that can be easily retrieved and manipulated without any concern for file size. The redesigned Access table has several features that enable you to store and manipulate data effortlessly.

The Field Insertion Feature

The *Field Insertion* feature in Access 2010 allows you to easily insert a new field by just typing the field name in the header row of a new column in the Datasheet view of a table. This feature is used to bypass the traditional process of using the Design view to insert a new field. This feature also enables you to create a table structure even if you are not familiar with the involutions of a database.

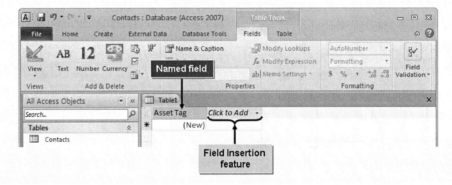

Figure 5-1: The tabbed table window displaying the option to add a field by using the field insertion feature.

The Rich Text Memo Property

The *rich text memo property* allows you to format data in tables. You can apply text formatting such as boldface, italics, and font color to individual characters or words in a rich text enabled memo field in the Datasheet view. You can use the **Memo Settings** option in the **Properties** group on the **Fields** tab to set the properties for a memo field. The property also has an **Append Only** property, which, when set, allows you to only add data to a memo field, but not modify the existing data.

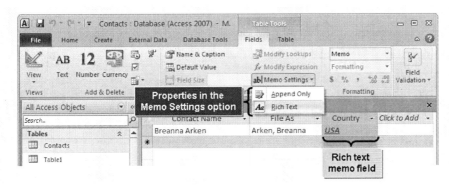

Figure 5-2: The rich text memo field options.

The Data Type Gallery

The *Data Type* gallery in Access 2010 allows you to add common field types such as Address and Currency to a table. It contains predefined fields that are organized into various sections. You can insert either a field or a group of fields with just a click, using **Quick Start** options. You can also add custom fields to predefined sections and save the modified predefined sections as new data types.

Data Types

A *data type* is a categorization of data associated with a particular field based on certain predefined characteristics. In addition to supporting the data types of earlier versions, Access 2010 supports the *Attachment data type*. This feature enables you to store external documents and binary files in a field and attach multiple files to a single record. Access 2010 automatically compresses some of the attached file types to optimize space.

Auto Calendar

Auto Calendar is an icon that is displayed to the right of the **Date/Time** data type field when you select the field. You can click this icon to select a date from the calendar that is displayed.

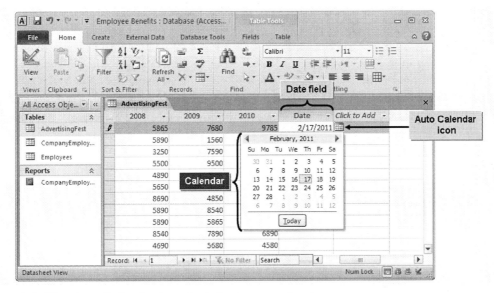

Figure 5-3: The Auto Calendar icon that displays a calendar.

Displaying the Auto Calendar Icon

To display the **Auto Calendar** icon for a **Date/Time** field, you need to enable the Auto Calendar feature by using the **Show Date Picker** property in the **Field Properties** section of the Design view. You can also turn off the Auto Calendar feature by setting the **Show Date Picker** property to **Never.**

The Allow Multiple Values Property

A **Lookup Wizard** is used to create fields that can store multiple values in a single field of a record by checking the **Allow Multiple Values** check box. You can also specify a field to store multiple values by setting the **Allow Multiple Values** property to **Yes** on the **Lookup** tab in the **Field Properties** pane of a field. You can either type the permissible values for the field or use values from a table or query result.

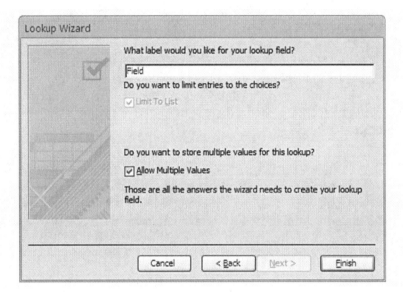

Figure 5-4: The Field Properties pane.

The Alternate Background Color Feature

Access supports the *alternate background color* feature that enables you to set alternate colors for every other row in a table. You can use this feature in the Datasheet view for tables, continuous forms, and reports, so that rows of a record are banded using the same color to enable easy identification of data.

How to Work with Tables

Procedure Reference: Create a Table in a Blank Database

To create a table in a blank database:

1. Launch the Microsoft Access 2010 application.
2. Create a database.
   - In the Backstage view, in the **Available Templates** pane, click **Blank database** and then click **Create** or;
   - In the Backstage view, in the **Available Templates** pane, double-click **Blank database.**
   - In the **Blank database** pane, in the **File name** text box, type a file name and Click **Create.**

 You can click the **Browse** button and navigate to the location where you want to create the database. You will then need to click **OK** in the **File New Database** dialog box.

Procedure Reference: Create and Add Fields to a Table

To create a table:

1. Open the database to create a table.
2. Save the table.
   a. Click the **Save** button on the Quick Access toolbar.
   b. In the **Save As** dialog box, in the **Table Name** text box, type a name for the table
   c. Click **OK.**
3. Add fields to the table.
   - Add a field using the Field Insertion feature.
     a. In the Datasheet view of the table, from the **Click to Add** drop-down list, select a data type and enter a field name.
     b. If necessary, press **Enter** to add another field.
   - Add a field using the Data Type gallery.
     a. On the **Table Tools** tab, on the **Fields** contextual tab, in the **Add & Delete** group, select the **More Fields** option to display the Data Type gallery.
     b. In the Data Type gallery, in the desired section, double-click the desired field names for the table.
4. Set the data type for a field.
   a. If necessary, switch to the Design view.
   b. In the table, click the **Data Type** column next to the desired field name, and from the drop-down list, select a data type.
5. Insert a record.
   - In the Datasheet view, in the table, specify the desired values in each row.
   - On the **Home** tab, in the **Records** group, click **New** to create a new record.

Procedure Reference: Create a Multivalued Field Manually

To create a multivalued field manually:

1. In the Design view, click the **Data Type** column next to the desired field name, and from the **Data Type** drop-down list, select **Lookup Wizard.**

2. Select the **I will type in the values that I want** option and click **Next.**

3. If necessary, in the **Number of columns** text box, specify the required number of columns to be displayed in the drop-down list for the column.

4. In the list box, specify the values that are acceptable for the field and click **Next.**

5. In the **What label would you like for your lookup field** text box, specify a name.

6. Check the **Allow Multiple Values** check box and click **Finish.**

7. Save the changes made to the table.

8. If necessary, in the **Microsoft Access** message box, click **Yes** to change the field type to enable storing multiple values.

Procedure Reference: Create a Multivalued Field by Using the Values from a Table or Query Result

To create a multivalued field by using the values from a table or query result:

1. In the Design view of the table, click the **Data Type** column next to the desired field, and from the **Data Type** drop-down list, select **Lookup Wizard.**

2. Select the **I want the lookup field to get the values from another table or query** option and click **Next.**

3. In the **View** section, select a view.

   ● Select **Tables** to view a list of all the tables in the database.

   ● Select **Queries** to view a list of all the queries in the database.

   ● Select **Both** to view a list of both the tables and queries in the database.

4. From the displayed view, select a table or query and click **Next.**

5. Add fields to be included in the Lookup column.

   ● In the **Available Fields** list box, select a field.

   ● Click the Add button to add the field to the **Selected Fields** list box.

   ● Click the Add all button to add all the fields in the **Available Fields** list box to the **Selected Fields** list box.

6. If necessary, remove fields from the **Selected Fields** list box.

   ● In the **Selected Fields** list box, select a field.

   ● Click the Remove button to remove the field from the **Selected Fields** list box.

   ● Click the Remove all button to remove all the fields from the **Selected Fields** list box.

7. Click **Next.**

8. On the **What sort order do you want for the items in your list box** page, from the **Ascending** drop-down list, select a field, click the toggle button to select a sort order and click **Next.**

9. If necessary, on the **How would you like the columns in your lookup field** page, adjust the width of the column and click **Next.**

10. In the **What label would you like for your lookup field** text box, specify the desired name.

11. Check the **Allow Multiple Values** check box and click **Finish.**

12. Save the changes made to the table.

13. If necessary, in the **Microsoft Access** message box, click **Yes** to change the data type field to store multiple values.

ACTIVITY 5-1
Creating a Table

Scenario:
Your client, Claire Connor, just called in to inform you that you are assigned a $20,000 project. However, this is only a prototype and further decisions will be made depending on the quality of the project. Because this is a high priority project, you want to allocate multiple resources for it. You decide to collate all information in one place so that it is available at short notice. You also want to create a database of projects that could be referenced later.

1. Create a table.

   a. Choose **Start→All Programs→Microsoft Office→Microsoft Access 2010** to launch the Microsoft Access 2010 application.

   b. In the Backstage view, verify that **New** is selected, and in the **Available Templates** pane, verify that **Blank database** is selected.

   c. In the **Blank database** pane, in the **File Name** text box, click and type *My Project Details*

   d. To the right of the **File Name** text box, click the **Browse** button.

   e. In the **File New Database** dialog box, navigate to the C:\084574Data\Working with Databases folder and click **OK.**

   f. In the **Blank database** pane, click **Create.**

   g. Observe that a database is created and a blank table is displayed.

   h. On the Quick Access toolbar, click the **Save** button.

   i. In the **Save As** dialog box, in the **Table Name** text box, type *Project* and click **OK.**

2. Create fields in the table.

   a. In the Project table, in the Datasheet view, from the **Click to Add** drop-down list, select **Text.**

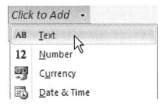

   b. In the **Field1** header, type *Project Name* and press **Tab.**

   c. From the **Click to Add** drop-down list, select **Text** to add another field header.

   d. Type *Employee Names* and press **Tab.**

e.   Similarly, add fields with the names *Date of Completion, Details,* and *Home Page.*

3.   Add another field to the header row.

    a.   On the **Table Tools Fields** contextual tab, in the **Add & Delete** group, from the **More Fields** drop-down list, in the **Number** section, select **Currency.**

    b.   In the **Field1** header, type *Current Value.*

4.   Set a data type for all the fields.

    a.   Select the **Home** tab, and in the **Views** group, from the **View** drop-down list, select **Design View.**

    b.   In the Project table, click the **Data Type** column next to **Date of Completion,** and from the **Data Type** drop-down list, select **Date/Time.**

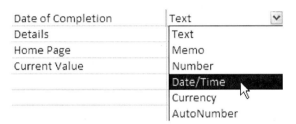

    c.   Click the **Data Type** column next to **Details,** and from the **Data Type** drop-down list, select **Memo.**

    d.   Click the **Data Type** column next to **Home Page,** and from the **Data Type** drop-down list, select **Hyperlink.**

5.   Create a multivalued field.

    a.   Click the **Data Type** column next to **Employee Names,** and from the **Data Type** drop-down list, select **Lookup Wizard.**

    b.   In the **Lookup Wizard,** select the **I will type in the values that I want** option and click **Next.**

    c.   In **Col1,** in the first cell, click and type *Josephine Riggs* and press **Tab.**

    d.   In the second cell, in the same column, type *Mike Allen*

    e.   Similarly, in the third and fourth cells of the same column, enter the names *Julia Barret* and *Beth Robinson,* respectively.

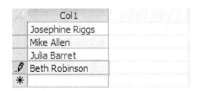

    f.   In the **Lookup Wizard,** click **Next.**

    g.   Check the **Allow Multiple Values** check box and click **Finish.**

    h.   In the **Microsoft Access** message box, click **Yes** to allow the Employee Names field to store multiple values.

i. On the Quick Access toolbar, click the **Save** button.

6. Insert a record.

   a. On the **Design** contextual tab, in the **Views** group, from the **View** drop-down list, select **Datasheet View.**

   b. In the Project table, in the first row, in the Project Name field, click and type ***Eastern Connection***

   c. Click the Employee Names field, and in the drop-down list, check the **Mike Allen** and **Julia Barret** check boxes and then click **OK.**

   d. Place the mouse pointer on the separator line between the Employee Names and Date of Completion headers, and when the mouse pointer changes to a double-headed arrow, double-click to increase the width of the Employee Names field.

   e. Observe that the Employee Names field now contains multiple employees' names.

   f. Press **Tab,** and next to the Date of Completion column, click the **Auto Calendar** icon.

   g. Navigate to and select a date that is six months from today.

   h. Similarly, enter the following information in the appropriate fields.
      - Details: This is a prototype.
      - Home Page: http://eastern.example
      - Current Value: 20000

7. Save and close the table and database.

   a. On the Quick Access toolbar, click the **Save** button

   b. Close the Project table tabbed window.

   c. Select the **File** tab and choose **Close Database.**

TOPIC B
Work with Queries and Macros

You created tables and are now ready to enter and edit data in tables. You can simplify working with tables by automating certain tasks or by combining information from multiple tables in a database. In this topic, you will work with queries and macros.

When working in a database, you may need to perform repetitive tasks such as inserting data into tables, analyzing information in tables, or generating reports. This may be time consuming and require additional effort. By creating and using queries and macros, you can automate these tasks and save valuable time and effort. Access 2010 has a new redesigned query and macro interface that helps you create queries and macros to accomplish common tasks quickly and efficiently.

Types of Queries

You can create several types of queries using the **Query Wizard** dialog box in Access.

Query Type	Used To
Simple	Select fields from multiple tables and query results.
Crosstab	Calculate and summarize data from tables and query results in a spreadsheet like format.
Find Duplicates	Find duplicate field values in a table or query result.
Find Unmatched	Find records in one table or query result that have no related records in another table or query result.

Advanced Querying Options

Advanced querying options such as *macros, modules,* and class modules can be accessed from the **Macros & Code** group on the **Create** tab. When you select the **Macro** option, the **Design** contextual tab is displayed. This tab contains various commands such as **Run, Expand Actions,** and **Action Catalog** under the groups **Tools, Collapse/Expand,** and **Show/Hide** for manipulating a macro. When you select the **Module** or **Class Module** option, the enhanced Microsoft *Visual Basic for Applications (VBA)* opens, where you can write code blocks for the module or class module.

Figure 5-5: *The advanced querying options available in the Macros & Code group.*

The Macro Designer

Macro Designer is a tool that enables you to create macros. The designer interface displays the **Add New Action** drop-down list that helps you build code blocks to add conditional statements and arguments. You can add a conditional statement or an argument by clicking the **Add New Action** drop-down list and selecting an action, or by double-clicking, or dragging an action from the **Action Catalog.** With Access 2010, you can use additional conditional statements. You can also perform other functions such as deleting an action or moving an action up or down one level in the Macro Designer. The buttons in the **Collapse/Expand** group provide you with a compact view of a macro.

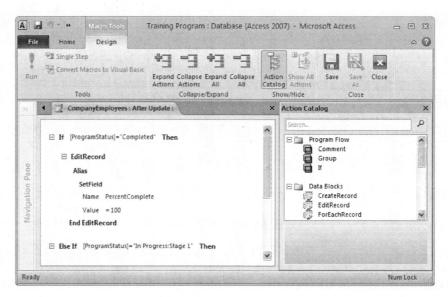

Figure 5-6: A macro created in the Macro Designer.

Data Macros

A *data macro* is a feature that allows you to attach macros to table data. You can create data macros using the Macro Designer. When you attach code snippets to the fields in a table or record, any changes made to the table will automatically execute that code snippet. The advantage of using data macros is that when you attach a data macro to a field, you can execute the same code snippet in other Access objects, such as forms and reports, that share that field, saving you from having to re-create the code snippet. However, data macros cannot process multivalued or attachment data types.

Embedded Macros

Embedded macros are macros that are part of the property attached to an event. Embedded macros can be accessed from the **Event** tab on the **Property Sheet.** They can be referenced from only the event property of the object they are attached to and not from the Navigation pane like data macros. Using the embedded macro feature, you can embed macros in events associated with a form, report, or control.

IntelliSense

The *IntelliSense* feature in Access 2010 allows you to effortlessly build expressions that you want to use in a given context by automatically displaying the expression as you type. As you build expressions, the IntelliSense feature displays a drop-down list from which you can select the expression you want to use. It also displays the complete declaration for the expression and a ScreenTip providing additional information about the selected expression. This feature is available in tables, queries, forms, and reports where expressions are used. The advantage of this feature is that it will help you minimize errors that may arise when working with long expressions and field names.

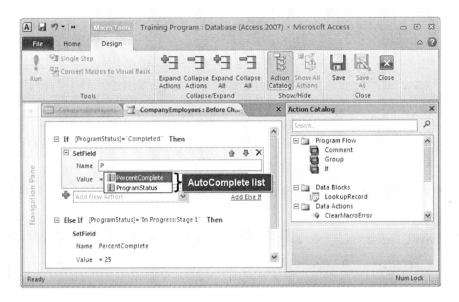

Figure 5-7: *Expressions displayed by the IntelliSense feature of a macro.*

The Expression Builder Dialog Box

The *Expression Builder* dialog box allows you to select database objects to build formulas and calculations that are used with queries and reports by using the application's built-in operators and functions. The improved **Expression Builder** interface in Access 2010 includes three columns that display expression elements, expression categories, and expression values.

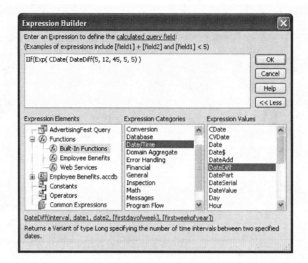

Figure 5-8: *Various expressions available in the Expression Builder dialog box.*

How to Work with Queries and Macros

Procedure Reference: Create a Simple Query

To create a simple query:

1. On the **Create** tab, in the **Queries** group, click the **Query Wizard** button.

2. In the **New Query** dialog box, verify that **Simple Query Wizard** is selected and click **OK.**

3. In the **Simple Query Wizard,** in the **Available fields** list, select the field you want to add and move it to the **Selected Fields** list and click **Next.**

4. In the **Simple Query Wizard,** select **Open the query to view information** option and click **Finish.**

Procedure Reference: Create and Run a Macro

To create and run a macro:

1. Open a database and display the table that you want to update using a macro.

2. On the **Table Tools Table** contextual tab, in the **After Events** group, click **After Update.**

3. Add a conditional statement.

    ● In the **Action Catalog** pane, in the **Program Flow** section, double-click **If** to add an If conditional statement block or;

    ● In the **Action Catalog** pane, in the **Program Flow** section, drag the **If** condition onto the **Add New Action** text box.

4. In the Macro Designer, in the **If** text box, type the condition statement.

5. Set a field value.

    a. In the **Action Catalog** pane, in the **Data Blocks** section, double-click **EditRecord** to add an **EditRecord** block to the Macro Designer.

    b. In the **Action Catalog,** pane in the **Data Actions** section, double-click **SetField** to add a **SetField** block to the Macro Designer.

    c. In the **Name** text box, type the desired name, and in the **Value** text box, type a value.

6.   Add another conditional statement.

    a.   Click the **If** statement to activate the **If** block and click the **Add Else If** link to add an Else If block.

    b.   In the **Else If** text box, type the desired expression.

    c.   Add the **EditRecord** action to add an EditRecord block.

7.   If necessary, add other action blocks as required.

8.   On the **Table Tools Design** contextual tab, click **Save** and then click **Close** to save the changes and close the Macro Designer.

9.   Navigate to the table and update the records as desired to execute the macro logic.

10.   If necessary, run the macro in a form.

    a.   On the **Create** tab, in the **Forms** group, from the **More Forms** drop-down list, select **Multiple Items.**

    b.   On the **Design** contextual tab, in the **Views** group, from the **View** drop-down list, select **Form View.**

    c.   Update the form record to run the macro.

ACTIVITY 5-2
Creating Macros to Update Table Data

Before You Begin:
The Microsoft Access 2010 application is open.

Scenario:
As the Human Resources manager of an organization, you need to keep track of the training programs that are assigned to the employees and update the completion status of the programs. You have the employee records listed in a table. You do not want to manually update the percentage of completion because this might be a time-consuming and tedious task. You decide to create a macro to automate the process.

---

1. Display the Macro Designer.

   a. Navigate to the C:\084574Data\Working with Databases folder and open the Training Program.accdb database.

   b. In the Navigation Pane, double-click the **CompanyEmployees** table to open it.

   c. Select the **Table Tools Table** contextual tab, and in the **Before Events** group, click **Before Change.**

   d. Observe that the Macro Designer is displayed along with the **Action Catalog** pane.

---

2. Add a conditional statement to a macro to perform an action.

   a. In the **Action Catalog** pane, in the **Program Flow** section, double-click **If** to add an If conditional statement block.

   b. In the **If** text box, type **P**

   c. Observe that the IntelliSense feature, which lists all the possible field names and functions that you may add as the criteria for the If condition, is activated.

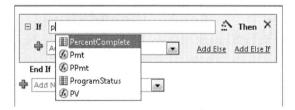

   d. In the AutoComplete list, double-click **ProgramStatus** to add it to the **If** text box and type *="Completed"*

---

3. Set a field value for the PercentComplete field.

   a. In the **Action Catalog** pane, in the **Data Actions** section, double-click **SetField** to add a **SetField** block.

---

b. In the **SetField** block, in the **Name** text box, type *P* and from the AutoComplete list, double-click **PercentComplete** and press **Tab.**

c. In the **Value** text box, type *100*

---

4. Set a field value for the ProgramStatus field.

a. Click the **Add Else If** link to add an **Else If** block.

b. In the **Else If** text box, type *P*

c. In the AutoComplete list box, double-click **ProgramStatus** to add it to the **Else If** text box and type *="In Progress:Stage 1"*

d. In the **Action Catalog** pane, in the **Data Actions** section, double-click **SetField** to add a **SetField** block.

e. In the **SetField** block, in the **Name** text box, type *P* and from the AutoComplete list, double-click **PercentComplete** and press **Tab.**

f. In the **Value** text box, type *25*

g. Click the **Add Else If** link to add an Else If condition to the macro designer.

h. In the **Else If** text box, type *P* and in the displayed drop-down list, double-click **ProgramStatus** to add it to the **If** text box and type *="In Progress:Stage 2"*

i. In the **Action Catalog** pane, in the **Data Actions** pane, double-click **SetField** to add a **SetField** block.

j. In the **SetField** block, in the **Name** text box, type *P* and from the **AutoComplete** list, double-click **PercentComplete** and press **Tab.**

    k.   In the **Value** text box, type *75*

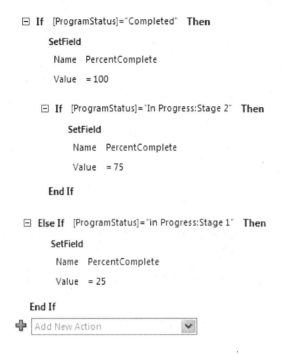

    l.   On the **Design** contextual tab, in the **Close** group, click **Save** and then click **Close** to save the changes and close the Macro Designer.

5.   Run the macro.

    a.   In the CompanyEmployees table tabbed window, in the first row, click the **ProgramStatus** field, and from the drop-down list, select **Completed** and then press **Tab** twice.

    b.   Observe that in the PercentComplete column, in the first row, the macro automatically updates the record.

    c.   Similarly, make changes to the next two rows and verify that the updates are automated to reflect the current status.

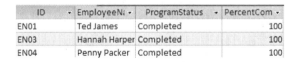

ID	EmployeeN:	ProgramStatus	PercentCom
EN01	Ted James	Completed	100
EN03	Hannah Harper	Completed	100
EN04	Penny Packer	Completed	100

6.   Save and close the database.

    a.   On the Quick Access toolbar, click the **Save** button to save the changes to the table.

    b.   Close the CompanyEmployees table tabbed window.

    c.   Save the database as *My Training Program.accdb* and close it.

TOPIC C
Create Forms

You worked with queries and macros to view and update table data. Manually updating data for a specific record in a table may take a lot of time and is prone to errors. Forms enable you to efficiently work with data in individual table records. In this topic, you will create forms.

If you are working with a large database, you may need to input several records, and this could prove to be a cumbersome process. However, forms enable you to efficiently add, view, edit, or delete data from tables easily resulting in increased productivity.

Form Creation Tools

You can create forms by using the form creation tools in the **Forms** group on the **Create** tab.

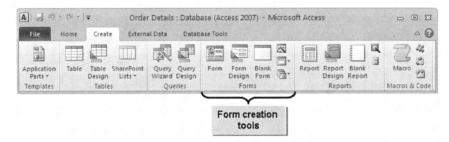

Figure 5-9: The form creation tools displayed in the Forms group.

Form Creation Tool	Enables You To
Form	Use fields in a table. The form is displayed in the Layout view. The form contains a subform that is dependent on data in a table or query if the table has a one-to-many relationship with another table. If the table has relationships defined with more than one table, the subform will not be created. The subform can be deleted.
Form Design	Create a form in the Design view.
Blank Form	Create a blank form that can be used to build a form from the beginning.
More Forms	Create additional forms such as: • **Multiple Items:** Allows you to generate a form that displays all the records in a table. • **Datasheet:** Allows you to create a form in the Datasheet view. • **Split Form:** Allows you to view a form simultaneously in the Form and Datasheet views. • **Modal Dialog:** Allows you to create a modal form with the **OK** and **Cancel** buttons enabled. • **PivotChart:** Allows you to create a form in the PivotChart view. • **PivotTable:** Allows you to create a form in the PivotTable view.

The WYSIWYG Interface

The *What You See Is What You Get (WYSIWYG)* interface allows you to modify the design layouts in a form even as you are working in it. In the Layout view, you can use the WYSIWYG interface to customize layouts, which will reduce the time and effort by eliminating the need to switch to the Design view each time you want to modify a form layout.

Layouts

Layouts are views of how controls appear in a form and enable you to make design changes to an interface element. In Access, you can set layouts for forms by using the **Form Layout Tools Arrange** contextual tab. Each layout consists of control margins that you can use to point out the location of information displayed within a control. Layouts also incorporate control padding, which is used to set spacing between gridlines on a form. Access allows you to create forms in two types of layouts: *tabular layouts* that display controls in a horizontal table format with one row per record and *stacked layouts* that display controls vertically.

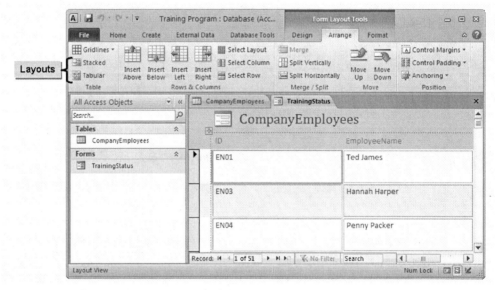

Figure 5-10: *The Layout options available in the Table group.*

The Anchoring Feature

The *anchoring* feature provides options that allow you to set the form elements at specific positions on a form. There are various anchoring options available, such as **Top Left, Stretch Down,** and **Bottom Left.** You can access this feature in the Layout view and Design view from the **Position** group on the **Form Design Tools Arrange** contextual tab.

The Property Sheet Pane

The *Property Sheet* pane contains all properties that you can set for controls in a form. The **Property Sheet** pane can be accessed from the **Arrange** tab on the **Form Design Tools** contextual tab. The tools in the **Property Sheet** pane are grouped into five functional tabs.

Tab	Used to Set Properties
Format	For text displayed on a control including font, color, line spacing, and text alignment.

Tab	Used to Set Properties
Data	For validating data in a field. You can set formats and input masks or restrict values entered in a field.
Event	For events that occur in a control.
Other	For tabs, AutoCorrect, and status bar.
All	Under all the categories.

The Application Parts Gallery

The *Application Parts* gallery lists database objects such as tables, queries, reports, and forms as templates. You can select a template from the **Blank Forms** section to add a specific form to a database, or you can use the **Quick Start** section to add database templates such as Comments, Contacts, Issues, Tasks, or Users. The **Contacts, Issues, Tasks,** and **Users** templates allow you to create a relationship with one or more parts of an existing database by importing database objects into the newly created database.

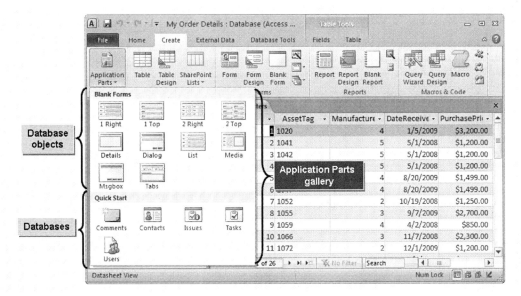

Figure 5-11: *The Application Parts gallery displaying the application templates available in Access 2010.*

How to Create Forms

Procedure Reference: Build a Form from Existing Table Data

To build a form from existing table data:

1. In the Navigation Pane, select a table.

2. On the **Create** tab, in the **Forms** group, select any of the options to generate a form.

    *   Select **Form** to create a form.

    *   Select **Form Design** to create a form and design it.

    *   Select **Blank Form** to create a blank form.

    *   Select **Form Wizard** to create a form using the wizard.

    *   Select **Navigation** to create a navigation form.

    *   Select **More Forms** and then select one of the other available form creation option.

3. If necessary, switch to the Form view to see the table data.

4. On the Quick Access toolbar, click the **Save** button.

5. In the **Save As** dialog box, in the **Form Name** text box, specify a name and click **OK.**

Procedure Reference: Modify Table Data Using a Form

To modify table data using a form:

1. Open a form.

2. Work with the form.

    *   In the form, navigate to a record and update the desired fields.

    *   Insert a new record.

        *   On the **Home** tab, in the **Records** group, click **New** and fill in the necessary fields or;

        *   On the **Record** navigation bar, click the **New (blank) record** button and fill in the necessary fields.

Procedure Reference: Build a Database Object Using the Application Parts Gallery

To build a database object by using the Application Parts gallery:

1. Open a blank database, and on the **Create** tab, in the **Templates** group, click **Application Parts.**

2. From the Application Parts gallery, select an application part.

    *   In the **Blank Forms** section, select a form to add to the database.

    *   In the **Quick Start** section, select an application part template, and in the **Create Relationship** wizard, specify the relationship to include in the database object.

3. Open the database object that is added and insert records and fields as required.

4. Save and close the database.

Procedure Reference: Design a Form Using a Form Layout

To design a form using a form layout:

1. Open a form.

2. Switch to the Layout view.

3. Arrange the form controls by selecting the control you want to move and dragging it to the desired location.

4. If necessary, add a background image.

   a. On the **Format** contextual tab, in the **Background** group, from the **Background Image** drop-down list, select **Browse.**

   b. In the **Insert Picture** dialog box, navigate to a folder, select the desired image, and click **OK.**

5. If necessary, format the controls by selecting options from the **Design, Arrange,** and **Format** contextual tabs.

6. Save the form.

ACTIVITY 5-3
Creating a Form Using Application Parts

Before You Begin:

The Access application is open.

Scenario:

You want to build a database of your contacts, but you do not have the time to create new tables and forms. So, you decide to use application parts to quickly create a form.

---

1. Add the **Contacts** application part to a database.

   a. Open a blank database.

   b. Select the **Create** tab, and in the **Templates** group, from the **Application Parts** drop-down list, in the **Quick Start** section, select **Contacts.**

   c. In the **Microsoft Access** message box, click **Yes** to close all open objects.

   d. Observe that the Contacts template is loaded and that related tables, queries, forms, and reports are displayed in the Navigation Pane.

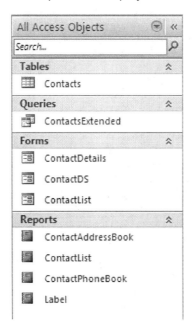

---

2. Enter the first name, last name, job title, and company name in the form.

   a. Double-click the **ContactDetails** form to open it.

   b. In the **First Name** text box, click and type *Breanna* and press **Tab.**

   c. In the **Last Name** text box, type *Arken* and press **Tab.**

   d. In the **Job Title** text box, type *Sales Rep* and press **Tab.**

e. In the **Company** text box, type *New World Properties* and then press **Tab** twice.

3. Enter other contact information.

a. In the **E-mail** text box, type *barken@ogc.com* and press **Tab.**

b. In the **Web Page** text box, type *barkenogc.com* and press **Tab.**

c. In the **Business Phone** text box, type *617–555–3698*

d. Similarly, type the information appended below in the respective fields.
    - Address: 145 Windsor Drive
    - City: Alexandria
    - State/Province: VA
    - Zip/Postal Code: 22314

e. On the Quick Access toolbar, click the **Save** button.

 Only the required information must be inserted into the form. The other fields must be left empty.

f. In the **Contact Details** form, click **Save & Close.**

4. Check whether the contact information is displayed in other database objects and save it.

a. In the Navigation Pane, double-click the **Contacts** table to open it.

b. Observe that the details entered in the form are auto populated in the table.

c. Double-click the **ContactList** report to view it.

d. Observe that the details on the report include the new data you entered in the form.

e. Right-click the Contact List report tab and choose **Close All** to close all the open windows.

5. Save and close the database.

a. Save the database as *My Contacts* in the C:\084574Data\Working with Databases folder.

b. Close the database.

TOPIC D
Create Reports

You created forms to streamline the data entry process. Although forms can be used to store data, you may, at times, require to extract selective data and present it in an easy to read format. In this topic, you will generate a report.

You may have to share information in a database with your clients. However, in the interest of the company, you may not be willing to share confidential information contained in the database, or you may want to specify the data display in a particular format to share the information. Such tasks are made easier with the redesigned report creation tools in Access 2010.

The Report Command

The *Report* command on the **Create** tab enables you to create reports quickly using data from a table or query result. You can manipulate the properties of a report by using the **Property Sheet** command in the **Tools** group on the **Design** contextual tab. While fields in a report can be grouped and sorted by using the **Group, Sort, and Total** pane, the formatting and layout of a report can be changed by using the **Format** and **Arrange** contextual tabs. You can also set the page layout for a report by using the **Page Setup** contextual tab..

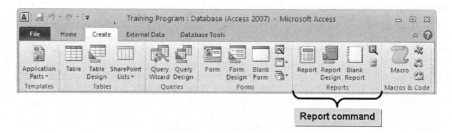

Figure 5-12: The Report command available in the Reports group.

Enhanced Sorting and Filtering Options

Data in reports can be sorted in either ascending or descending order, based on the information contained in the respective fields. You can also sort data ranging from the smallest to the largest and from the oldest to the newest records by launching the **Group, Sort, and Total** pane or by using the right-click contextual menu. Moreover, you can filter data based on the data type in a field. *Filters* are available in all the views that display data. You can filter data to display only the records that match your criteria. You can apply different types of filters, such as text filters for textual data, number filters for numerical data, and date filters for the date and time data.

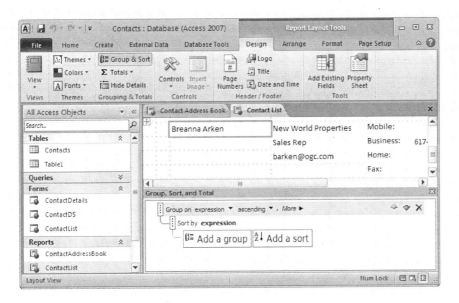

Figure 5-13: *The Group & Sort option used to sort and filter data.*

The Totals Feature

The *Totals* feature is used to add a Totals row to a report. This feature can be accessed from the **Grouping & Totals** group on the **Design** contextual tab. It provides options for calculating the sum, average, count of records, count of values, maximum, minimum, standard deviation, and variance of data in a field.

Enhanced Conditional Formatting Options

Conditional formatting is a formatting technique that applies a specified format to a cell or a range of cells based on a set of predefined criteria and the data contained in that cell. The **Conditional Formatting Rules Manager** dialog box allows you to set the condition for formatting by using the default rules or customized rules, and preview the effects of the selection before applying them. Conditional formatting in Access 2010 supports data bars that enable you to visually depict data.

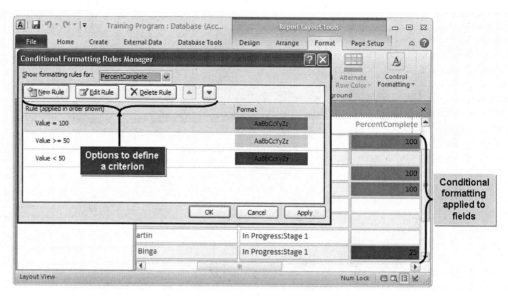

Figure 5-14: *The Conditional Formatting Rules Manager dialog box.*

Printing Reports with Conditional Formatting

You may want to print reports that have conditional formatting applied to them. To get the best results out of such reports, ensure that you apply a formatting style that will highlight the information you want displayed in print. For example, if you have a color printer, you can highlight key information by using color formatting rules, but its effect will be lost if you use a black and white printer.

How to Create Reports

Procedure Reference: Generate a Report Using the Report Wizard

To generate a report using the **Report Wizard:**

1. Select the table or query that you want to use for the report.

2. On the **Create** tab, in the **Reports** group, click **Report Wizard.**

3. On the **Which fields do you want on your report** page, in the **Available Fields** list box, double-click the desired fields to add them to the **Selected Fields** list box and click **Next.**

4. On the **Do you want to add any grouping levels** page, select a grouping option and click **Next** to add the fields by grouping them.

5. On the **What sort order do you want for your records** page, specify the order in which the fields will be displayed in your report and click **Next.**

6. On the **How would you like to lay out your report** page, select a layout option and click **Next.**

7. On the **What title do you want for your report** page, enter a report name and click **Finish.**

8. Close the **Print Preview** page.

9. Save the changes made to the report.

Procedure Reference: Group and Sort Data in a Report

To group and sort data in a report:

1. Open a report and switch to the Layout view.

2. On the **Report Layout Tools Design** contextual tab, in the **Grouping & Totals** group, select the **Group & Sort** option.

3. Group the data.

    a. In the **Group, Sort, and Total** pane, click **Add a Group.**

    b. From the **Group On Select Field** drop-down list, select the field that you want to use to group the data.

4. Sort the data.

    a. From the **Sort by select field** drop-down list, select the field on which data has to be sorted.

    b. In the **Sort by** pane, from the drop-down list that appears next to the item to be sorted, select a sort option to sort in either ascending or descending order, or from the smallest to the largest value.

    c. If necessary, specify a sort order for other fields in the report.

5. If necessary, print the report.

6. Save and close the report.

Procedure Reference: Add a Total Using the Totals Command

To add a total using the **Totals** command:

1. Open a report and switch to the Layout view.

2. If necessary, select the **Report Layout Tools Design** contextual tab.

3. In the report window, select a column.

4. In the **Grouping & Totals** group, click **Totals** and select the desired total option.

5. If necessary, print the report.

6. Save and close the report.

Procedure Reference: Filter Data in a Report

To filter data in a report:

1. Open a report and switch to the Layout view.

2. In the report tabbed window, select the field based on which you want to filter data

3. On the **Home** tab, in the **Sort & Filter** group, click **Filter.**

4. From the drop-down list that appears, deselect the options that are not required and click **OK.**

5. If necessary, print the report.

6. Save and close the report.

Procedure Reference: Apply Conditional Formatting to a Report

To apply conditional formatting to a report:

1. Open a report in the Layout view.

2. On the **Report Layout Tools Format** contextual tab, in the **Control Formatting** group, click **Conditional Formatting.**

3. In the **Conditional Formatting Rules Manager** dialog box, click **New Rule** to add a new rule.

4. In the **New Formatting Rule** dialog box, select a rule type.

   ● Select **Check values in the current record or use an expression,** and in the **Format only cells where the** section, choose an appropriate rule or;

   ● Select **Compare to other records,** and in the **Data bar format settings** section, choose an appropriate rule.

5. In the **New Formatting Rule** dialog box, click **OK** to close it.

6. If necessary, in the **Conditional Formatting Rules Manager** dialog box, select a rule and click the **Edit Rule** button to edit the rule.

7. If necessary, in the **Conditional Formatting Rules Manager** dialog box, select a rule and click the **Delete Rule** button to delete the rule.

8. In the **Conditional Formatting Rules Manager** dialog box, click **Apply** and then click **OK** to apply conditional formatting to the report and close the dialog box.

Procedure Reference: Apply Conditional Formatting to a Report Using Data Bars

To apply conditional formatting to a report using data bars:

1. Open a report in the Layout view.

2. On the **Form Design Tools Format** contextual tab, in the **Control Formatting** group, click **Conditional Formatting.**

3. In the **Conditional Formatting Rules Manager** dialog box, click **New Rule** to add a new rule.

4. In the **New Formatting Rule** dialog box, in the **Select a rule type** section, select the **Compare to other records** option.

5. In the **Data bar format settings** section, choose an appropriate rule.

   ● From the **Type** drop-down list, select a data bar type.

   ● From the **Value** drop-down list, select a data bar value.

   ● From the **Bar color** drop-down list, select a data bar color.

6. Click **OK** to close the **New Formatting Rule** dialog box.

7. In the **Conditional Formatting Rules Manager** dialog box, click **Apply** and then click **OK** to apply conditional formatting to the report and close the dialog box.

ACTIVITY 5-4
Creating a Formatted Report

Data Files:

C:\084574Data\Working with Databases\Employee Benefits.accdb

Before You Begin:
The Access application is open.

Scenario:
One of the highlights of your company's corporate programs is the Annual AdvertisingFestival that is held every year. You want to determine the popularity of each participant booth by examining the sales leads generated at each booth. You decide to display this information as a visual by using data bars.

---

1. Enter the details of the report in the **Report Wizard.**

    a. Navigate to the C:\084574Data\Working with Databases folder and open the Employee Benefits.accdb database.

    b. In the Navigation Pane, select the **AdvertisingFest** table.

    c. On the **Create** tab, in the **Reports** group, click **Report Wizard.**

    d. In the **Report Wizard,** in the **Tables/Queries** drop-down list, verify that **Table: AdvertisingFest** is selected and click the Add all button.

    e. In the **Selected Fields** list box, select the **ID** field and click the Remove button to remove the ID field and click **Next.**

    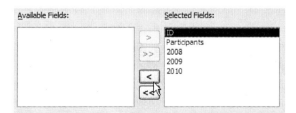

    f. On the **Do you want to add any grouping levels** page, click **Next** to add the fields without grouping them.

---

g. On the **What sort order do you want for your records** page, from the drop-down list, select **Participants** and click **Next.**

h. On the **How would you like to lay out your report** page, in the **Layout** section, verify that **Tabular** is selected and click **Next.**

i. On the **What title do you want for your report** page, in the text box, double-click the existing text and type *AdvertisingFestival*

j. Verify that the **Preview the report** option is selected and click **Finish.**

k. Observe that the report displays the selected fields.

l. On the **Print Preview** tab, in the **Close Preview** group, click the **Close Print Preview** button.

2. Format the data in the report.

   a. Verify that the report is displayed in the Design view.

   b. In the **Report Header** section, click the text "AdvertisingFestival" to select it.

   c. Select the **Report Design Tools Format** contextual tab, and in the **Font** group, from the **Font** drop-down list, select **Arial.**

   d. From the **Font Color** gallery, in the **Standard Colors** section, select the **Maroon** color, which is the sixth color in the first row.

   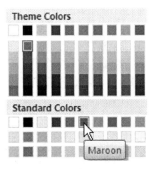

3. Format the page layout.

   a. Select the **Page Setup** contextual tab, and in the **Page Size** group, from the **Size** drop-down list, select **Legal.**

   b. In the **Page Size** group, from the **Margins** drop-down list, select **Normal.**

4. Apply data bar settings.

a. On the status bar, click the **Layout View** button to change to the Layout view.

b. In the AdvertisingFestival report, in the first row, in the first column, click the cell containing the value "5890."

c. On the **Format** contextual tab, in the **Control Formatting** group, click **Conditional Formatting.**

d. In the **Conditional Formatting Rules Manager** dialog box, in the **Show formatting rules for** drop-down list, verify that **2008** is selected and click **New Rule.**

e. In the **New Formatting Rule** dialog box, in the **Select a rule type** section, select the **Compare to other records** option and click **OK.**

f. From the **Show formatting rules for** drop-down list, select **2009.**

g. In the **Microsoft Access** message box, click **Continue and Apply Changes** to continue applying the rules.

h. Verify that 2009 is selected in the **Show formatting rules for** drop-down list.

i. In the **Conditional Formatting Rules Manager** dialog box, click **New Rule.**

j. In the **New Formatting Rule** dialog box, in the **Select a rule type** section, select the **Compare to other records** option and click **OK.**

k. From the **Show formatting rules for** drop-down list, select **2010.**

l. In the **Microsoft Access** message box, click **Continue and Apply Changes** to continue applying the rules.

m. Similarly, add the data bar rule for the year 2010.

n. In the **Conditional Formatting Rules Manager** dialog box, click **Apply** and click **OK** to apply the data bar settings for the year 2010.

o. Observe that the data bars represent the sales leads generated by the booths over the last three years.

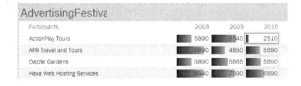

---

5. Save and close the database.

a. On the Quick Access toolbar, click the **Save** button.

b. In the AdvertisingFestival report tabbed window, click the **Close** button.

c. Save the database as *My Employee Benefits.accdb* and close it.

TOPIC E
Work with External Data

You generated reports to present data in an easy to read format. You may want to export the report data to other file formats, or import the data contained in other applications into Access to process data. In this topic, you will work with external data.

Most companies use a wide variety of applications and file formats in their work environment. However, some users may not have the Office suite installed on their systems. In such circumstances, you should be able to convert Access data into other file formats and integrate external data into your Access databases to collaborate with different types of users. The enhanced features in Access 2010 makes working with external data an easy task.

Import Options

Access provides you with *options for importing data* from various data sources such as Excel spreadsheets, ODBC databases, text files, XML files, SharePoint lists, data services, HTML documents, Outlook folders, or dBASE files. The commands in the **Import & Link** group on the **External Data** tab enable you to import data with the help of user-friendly wizards.

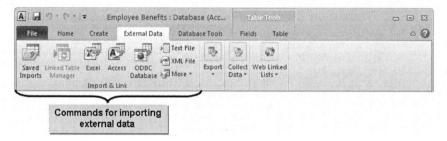

Figure 5-15: *The options available in the Import & Link group for importing data into Access.*

While importing data from sources such as an Excel worksheet, an HTML page, or a text file, you can specify a data storage option. Storage options include importing data into a new table, appending copies of records into a specified table, or linking to a data source by using a linked table. You can also save the import steps so that you do not need to run through the steps again to import data.

The Collect Data Group

The commands in the **Collect Data** group on the **External Data** tab allow you to collect and update external data via email by using Outlook 2010.

Export Options

Access provides you with various options for exporting data from Access to different file formats such as Excel spreadsheets, text files, XML files, PDF or XPS files, email, Access databases, Word, SharePoint lists, ODBC databases, HTML documents, or dBASE files. The commands in the **Export** group on the **External Data** tab are used to export Access data with the help of user-friendly wizards. While exporting data to formats such as Excel or a text file, you can not only specify the file format, but also retain most of the formatting and layout of different Access objects in the destination file. You can also save the export steps so that you do not need to run through them when you need to export the data again.

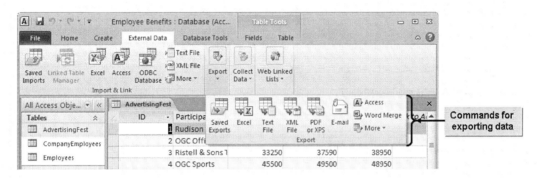

Figure 5-16: *The options available in the Export group for exporting data.*

SharePoint Lists

By using the commands in the **SharePoint Lists** group on the **External Data** tab, you can synchronize data between Access 2010 and a SharePoint server so that remote users can access the required files and work in a collaborative environment.

How to Work with External Data

Procedure Reference: Specify the Source and Destination of the Data to Be Imported

To specify the source and destination of the data to be imported:

1. Open the required database.

2. On the **External Data** tab, in the **Import & Link** group, select the file format of the source file.

3. In the **Get External Data - [Source Data Type]** dialog box, in the **Specify the source of the data** section, click the **Browse** button and navigate to the desired location.

4. In the **File Open** dialog box, select the source file and click **Open.**

5. In the **Specify how and where you want to store the data in the current database** section, select an option.

    *   Select the **Import the source data into a new table in the current database** option to create a table in the current database.

    *   Select the **Append a copy of the records to the table** option, and from the drop-down list, select a table to add records to an existing table in the database.

    *   Select the **Link to the data source by creating a linked table** option to create a table that retains its links to source data.

6. Click **OK.**

7. In the **Import [Source Data Type] Wizard** message box, click **OK.**

Procedure Reference: Import Data from an Excel Worksheet

To import data from an Excel worksheet:

1. Open the required database.

2. Specify the source from where the Excel data has to be imported.

3. In the **Import Spreadsheet Wizard,** in the **Your spreadsheet file contains more than one worksheet or range. Which worksheet or range would you like** section, select the data to be imported.

    *   Select the **Show Worksheets** option to import data from a worksheet.

    *   Select the **Show Named Ranges** option to import named ranges from a worksheet.

4. In the list box, select the table to be imported and click **Next.**

5. If necessary, check the **First Row Contains Column Headings** check box and click **Next.**

6. If necessary, specify the field options.

    *   In the **Field Name** text box, type the name of the field.

    *   From the **Indexed** drop-down list, select the option to specify whether the field is to be indexed.

    *   From the **Data Type** drop-down list, select a data type.

    *   Check the **Do not import field (Skip)** check box to ignore the field when data is imported.

7. In the **Import Spreadsheet Wizard,** click **Next.**

8. If necessary, specify the primary key.

    *   Select the **Let Access add primary key** option to automatically add a primary key.

    *   Select the **Choose my own primary key** option, and from the drop-down list, select an option to specify the desired field as the primary key.

    *   Select the **No primary key** option if you do not want to specify a primary key for the table.

9. In the **Import Spreadsheet Wizard** dialog box, click **Next.**

10. In the **Import To Table** text box, specify a name for the table and click **Finish** to import the data into a new table.

11. If necessary, check the **Save Import Steps** check box to save the import steps.

- In the **Save as** text box, specify the name of the import operation that is to be saved.

- In the **Description** text box, describe the function of the import operation.

- In the **Create an Outlook Task** section, check **Create Outlook Task** to create an Outlook task.

- In the **Get External Data-Excel Spreadsheet** dialog box, click **Save Import.**

Procedure Reference: Export Data to a Text File

To export data to a text file:

1. Open a database.

2. Specify the database object from which you want to export data.

3. On the **External Data** tab, in the **Export** group, click **Text File** to export the data in the text format.

4. In the **Export - Text File** dialog box, in the **Specify the destination file name and format** section, click **Browse** and navigate to the desired location.

5. Specify an export option.

- Check **Export data with formatting and layout** to export data with the formatting and layout options intact.

- Check **Open the destination file after the export operation is complete** to view the text file after the export.

- Check **Export only the selected records** to export only the selected records.

 You need to select the records that you want to export if you select the **Export only the selected records** option.

6. Click **OK.**

7. In the **Encode** dialog box, select an encoding option and click **OK.**

8. If necessary, save and close the text file.

9. If necessary, check **Save Export Steps** to quickly repeat the export process without using the wizard.

   a. In the **Save as** text box, specify the name of the export operation to be saved.

   b. If necessary, in the **Description** text box, describe the function of the export operation.

   c. If necessary, in the **Create an Outlook Task** section, check **Create Outlook Task** to create an Outlook task to remind you when it is time to repeat the export operation again.

   d. Click **Save Export.**

ACTIVITY 5-5
Importing and Exporting Data

Data Files:

C:\084574Data\Working with Databases\Order Details.accdb, C:\084574Data\Working with Databases\Computers.xlsx

Scenario:

Your colleague has sent you an Excel workbook that contains details about the various orders placed by customers. You want to create a database using this information. However, you do not want to type the data all over again. Also, because you are planning to go on vacation, your colleagues have volunteered to follow up on your contacts while you are away. You want to share your contact information database with them, but they do not have Access installed on their systems.

---

1. Specify the source of the Excel worksheet to be imported into Access 2010.

   a. From the C:\084574Data\Working with Databases folder, open the Order Details.accdb database.

   b. Select the **External Data** tab, and in the **Import & Link** group, click **Excel.**

   c. In the **Get External Data - Excel Spreadsheet** dialog box, in the **Specify the source of the data** section, click **Browse.**

   d. In the **File Open** dialog box, navigate to the C:\084574Data\Working with Databases folder.

   e. Select the **Computers.xlsx** file and click **Open.**

   f. Verify that the **Import the source data into a new table in the current database** option is selected and click **OK.**

---

2. Import data into the Access database.

   a. In the Import Spreadsheet Wizard, verify that the **First Row Contains Column Headings** check box is checked and that the records are displayed below. Click **Next.**

   b. In the **Field Options** section, in the **Field Name** text box, verify that **AssetTag** is displayed and also verify that its data type is **Text.**

   c. In the list box, click the **ManufacturerID** header, and in the **Field Options** section, from the **Data Type** drop-down list, select **Integer.**

   d. Click the headings for **DateReceived, PurchasePrice, Warranty,** and **EmployeeID** to review the data type that will be used for each heading and then click **Next.**

   e. Select the **Choose my own primary key** option and verify that **AssetTag** is selected and then click **Next.**

   f. In the **Import to Table** text box, verify that **tblComputers** is displayed and click **Finish.**

g. On the **Save Import Steps** page, verify that the check box is unchecked and click **Close.**

h. Double-click the **tblComputers** table to open it.

i. View the records and close the **tblComputers** table.

3. Specify the destination to export data.

a. Double-click the **Contacts:Table** table to open it.

b. On the **External Data** tab, in the **Export** group, click **Text File.**

c. In the **Export - Text File** wizard, in the **Specify the destination file name and format** section, observe the destination file name.

4. Set the export options and export data into a text file.

a. In the **Specify export options** section, check the **Export data with formatting and layout** check box.

b. Check the **Open the destination file after the export operation is complete** check box and click **OK.**

c. In the **Encode 'Contacts:Table' As** dialog box, verify that the **Windows (default)** option is selected and click **OK.**

d. Observe that the text file opens with the data that you exported from Access and close it.

```
-----------------------------------------------------
|  Customer ID   |               Company Name        |
-----------------------------------------------------
| QUICK          | AFR Tours                         |
-----------------------------------------------------
| FRANR          | MultiCor International            |
-----------------------------------------------------
| TRAIH          | OGC Advertising                   |
-----------------------------------------------------
| SPLIR          | Rudison Technologies Ltd.         |
-----------------------------------------------------
| LACOR          | LearnMark                         |
-----------------------------------------------------
```

e. On the **Save Export Steps** page, verify that the check box is unchecked and click **Close.**

f. Close the **Contacts:Table** table.

5. Save and close the database.

a. Save the database as *My Order Details.accdb*

b. Close the database.

TOPIC F
Design a Database for the Web

You imported data from other applications to work in Access and exported information from Access to other formats. To work with a database on the web and enable other users to view the database, you need to design web-specific tables, forms, queries, and reports. In this topic, you will build a database for the web.

Businesses today are connected to a global network and sharing information with users across boundaries is vital to their smooth functioning. The smartest way to achieve this is to make information available in a real-time environment. Access 2010 provides you with new design tools that enable you to create a database that is easily accessible through a web browser. Understanding the design requirements for a web-specific database will ensure that you can create a database that holds up-to-date information anytime, anywhere.

Web Objects

Web objects refer to database objects such as tables, forms, queries, and reports in a web database. These objects can be created only in Access 2010 and are indicated by a small globe icon within a database object's icon. Web objects generally cannot reference *client objects;* however, they can reference other web objects. All the functional elements of a client object are not visible on the web objects. For example, tables in a web database do not support the Design view and can be displayed only in the Datasheet view.

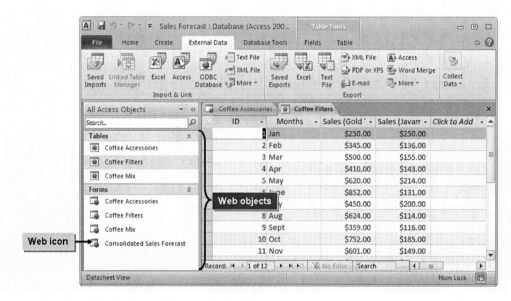

Figure 5-17: A table displayed in a web database.

The Web Compatibility Checker Feature

The *Web Compatibility Checker* feature enables you to identify whether the web database objects that you create are supported on the web. Before publishing a database to the web, you must run the web compatibility checker to ensure that the contents such as text, images, or controls in the database are presented consistently. If a database is not compatible for the web and you run this feature, Access displays a list of errors along with their descriptions and suggested resolutions.

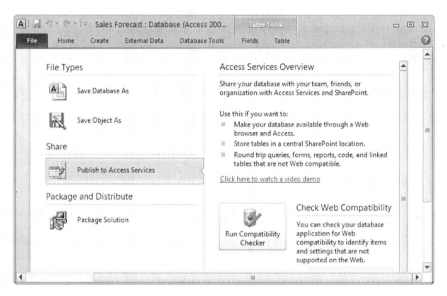

Figure 5-18: *The Run Compatibility Checker button in the Backstage view that helps you identify web compatibility issues.*

Navigation Forms

A *navigation form* is a layout that allows you to navigate within objects such as tables and forms within a web database. It provides you with easy navigation controls when working with Access web databases. There are six predefined navigation form layouts that are available by default in Access 2010. Once you add a navigation layout to the user interface, you can add controls and customize the layout according to your requirements. However, these controls can hold only Access forms and reports.

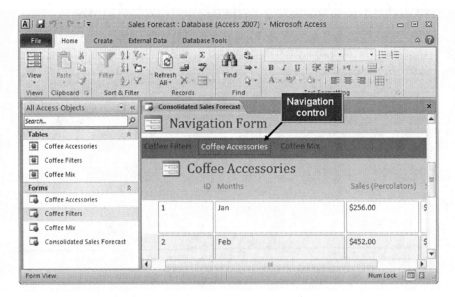

Figure 5-19: A navigation form displaying a control and subcontrol.

Web Browser Control

A *Web Browser Control* is a tool that allows you to view web content within the Access 2010 application. Selecting the **Web Browser Control** displays the **Insert Hyperlink** dialog box, where you can enter the URL of the website that you want to display in a database. This tool can be used only when you work with a web database form in the Form or Layout view.

Figure 5-20: A website inserted into a form using the Web Browser Control tool.

How to Design a Database for the Web

Procedure Reference: Create a Blank Web Database

To create a blank web database:

1. In the Backstage view, in the **Available Templates** pane, click **Blank web database.**
2. In the **Blank web database** section, in the **File name** text box, type a file name.
3. If necessary, click the **Browse** button and navigate to the location where the database will be created.
4. In the **File New Database** dialog box, click **OK.**
5. In the **Blank web database** section, click **Create** to display a blank table.

Procedure Reference: Add Fields and Records to a Table in a Web Database

To add fields and records to a table in a web database:

1. Create a table in a web database and save it with the desired name.
2. Add fields to the table by using the Field Insertion feature or the Data Type gallery.
3. Add a new record.
    a. On the **Home** tab, in the **Records** group, click **New** to create a new record.
    b. In the new record, specify the desired values in each field.
    c. If necessary, add more records to the table.

Procedure Reference: Build a Form in a Web Database

To build a form in a web database:

1. Open a table in a web database and on the **Create** tab, in the **Forms** group, click a form type to generate a form.
2. If necessary, on the **Design** contextual tab, in the **Controls** group, select a control tool and drag it to the form to add a control to the form.
3. Save the form.

Procedure Reference: Add a Navigation Form to a Web Form

To add a navigation form to a web form:

1. If necessary, create a blank web form.
2. On the **Create** tab, in the **Forms** group, from the **Navigation** drop-down list, select a navigation layout.
3. Drag a form or report from the Navigation Pane to the **Add New** navigation control.

Procedure Reference: Add a Web Browser Control to a Web Form

To add a web browser control to a web form:

1. Open the form in which you want to add a web browser control and if necessary, display the form in the Design or Layout view.
2. On the **Design** contextual tab, in the **Controls** group, click **Web Browser Control.**
3. On the form, click where you want the web page to be displayed.
4. In the **Insert Hyperlink** dialog box, in the **Address** text box, type the address of the web page you want to display in your database and press **Enter.**

ACTIVITY 5-6
Building a Tabbed Navigation Form in a Web Database

Data Files:

C:\084574Data\Working with Databases\Sales Forecast.accdb

Before You Begin:

The Access application is open.

Scenario:

You want to share the database of your department's sales forecast with the sales team in Asia. You also want to view information that is displayed on the company's website from the database and navigate through all the forms in your database.

---

1. Build forms by using table data.

   a. Navigate to the C:\084574Data\Working with Databases folder and open the Sales Forecast.accdb database.

   b. In the Navigation Pane, select the **Coffee Mix** table.

   c. Select the **Create** tab, and in the **Forms** group, click **Multiple Items.**

   d. On the Quick Access toolbar, click the **Save** button.

   e. In the **Save As** dialog box, in the **Form Name** text box, verify that Coffee Mix is displayed, and click **OK.**

   f. In the form's tabbed window, click the **Close** button.

   g. Similarly, create forms by using the Coffee Filters and Coffee Accessories tables and save them.

---

2. Create a blank form and add a navigation form layout to it.

   a. Select the **Create** tab, and in the **Forms** group, from the **Navigation** drop-down list, select the **Horizontal Tabs, 2 Levels** form to create a blank form.

   b. Observe that the navigation controls are added to the blank form and close the **Field List** pane.

   c. In the **Navigation Form** tabbed window, in the first **Add New** text place holder, double-click and type *Total Sales* and then press **Enter.**

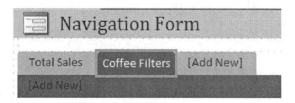

---

3. Add data to the navigation form.

a. In the Navigation Pane, click the **Coffee Filters** form and drag it to the Add New tab below the Total Sales tab.

b. Similarly, click the **Coffee Accessories** and **Coffee Mix** forms and drag them to the **Add New** tab that is located next to the Coffee Filters tab.

4. Add the **everythingforcoffee** web page to a form.

a. To the right of the Total Sales tab, in the **Add New** text place holder, double-click and type *More Info*

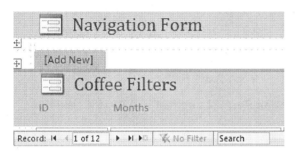

b. On the **Design** contextual tab, in the **Controls** group, click **Web Browser Control.**

c. In the **Navigation Form** tabbed window, click the **More Info** tab to display the **Insert Hyperlink** dialog box.

d. In the **Insert Hyperlink** dialog box, in the **Address** text box, type *www.everythingforcoffee.com* and press **Enter.**

e. Close the everythingforcoffee pop-up window.

f. Observe that the **everythingforcoffee** web page is displayed at the top half of the More Info tabbed window.

5. View the form in the tabbed window.

a. Switch to the Form view.

b. Close the everythingforcoffee pop-up window.

c. Select the **Total Sales** tab.

d. Observe that the **everythingforcoffee** website is displayed at the top half of the tabbed window, while the Coffee Filters, Coffee Accessories, and Coffee Mix forms are displayed at the bottom of the tabbed window.

e. Select the **Coffee Accessories** tab and scroll down to view the sales forecast of coffee accessories.

---

6. Save the form and close the database.

a. On the Quick Access toolbar, click the **Save** button.

b. In the **Save As** dialog box, in the **Form Name** text box, type *Consolidated Sales Forecast* and click **OK.**

c. Close the Consolidated Sales Forecast form.

d. Close the database.

e. Exit the Access 2010 application.

Lesson 5 Follow-up

In this lesson, you identified the new and enhanced features of Access 2010. You can now effectively create and design databases, record and analyze information, and extract data for distribution in various formats using the new and enhanced features.

1. What enhanced features do you prefer to use while generating reports?

2. How do you think the ability of Access 2010 to import and export data in other formats will help you in your work?

6 Managing Information at Work with Microsoft Outlook 2010

Lesson Time: 45 minutes

Lesson Objectives:

In this lesson, you will manage tasks using the new features in Microsoft Outlook 2010.

You will:

- Manage email messages.
- Locate information quickly.
- Share calendar information.
- Share contact information.
- Add RSS feeds.

Introduction

You represented information and statistical data in different formats and worked with databases. In an organization, in addition to working on different data and reports, it is important to share data with others. In this lesson, you will work with Outlook 2010.

Communication with peers and clients is an integral part of working in any organization. You probably managed your daily tasks using Outlook 2003 and are now migrating to Outlook 2010. The options in the 2010 interface are user friendly, making it much easier to manage, locate, and prioritize information.

TOPIC A
Manage Email Messages

You worked with databases in Access to store information. In addition to storing information, you will have to share information and correspond with others. In this topic, you will manage email messages using Outlook 2010.

Using Outlook, you can quickly and efficiently send information in a email message. There are times when you may also find it necessary to alter the content of a message. Perhaps, you may want to emphasize some text within the body of the message or correct a misspelled word. Outlook provides you with new tools to ensure that your messages are both accurate and easy to read.

Quick Steps

Quick steps are commands that facilitate some of the common tasks that would traditionally involve multiple actions, but can now be performed in a single click. They are displayed in the **Quick Steps** group on the **Home** tab. There are various default quick steps available for common tasks performed in Outlook. You can also create custom quick steps by using the **Create New** command, which displays the **Edit Quick Step** dialog box. You can edit, customize, or delete quick steps using the options in the **Manage Quick Steps** dialog box.

Figure 6-1: Quick steps displayed on the Home tab.

Default Quick Steps

Some of the default quick steps include:

- **Move To:** Marks an email message as read and moves it to a specified folder.
- **Reply & Delete:** Creates a reply message to an email and deletes the original message.
- **Done:** Marks an email message as complete and moves it to a specified folder.
- **Team E-mail:** Forwards an email message to your team members, as specified in the Address Book.
- **To Manager:** Forwards an email message to your manager, as specified in the Address Book.

The Manage Quick Steps Dialog Box

The **Manage Quick Steps** dialog box allows you to manage quick steps. You can also add shortcut keys and display ScreenTips for a quick step.

Component	Description
The **Quick step** drop-down menu	Displays all the quick steps such as **Move to, To Manager, Team E-mail, Done, Reply & Delete,** and **Create New.**
The **Description** section	Displays a description including the **Actions, Shortcut key,** and ScreenTip for a selected quick step.
The up and down arrow buttons	Provide options to navigate between the quick steps, and reorder their display in the **Quick step** list box.
The **New** drop-down list	Displays options to add a new quick step.
The **Edit** button	Allows you to edit a quick step.
The **Duplicate** button	Creates a duplicate quick step.
The **Delete** button	Allows you to delete a quick step.
The **Reset to Defaults** button	Resets quick steps to the default settings.

The Conversation View

In Outlook, email messages that share the same subject can be displayed together as a *conversation.* The messages in a conversation are arranged with the newest message placed on top in the View pane. When there is a response to the email in a conversation thread, that particular message is also moved to the top of the conversation. Message threads can be expanded or collapsed. The Conversation view is displayed in the folders where you saved messages and can be identified with an icon showing multiple envelopes. Conversations are useful when multiple ideas on a specific subject are exchanged among multiple senders and receivers.

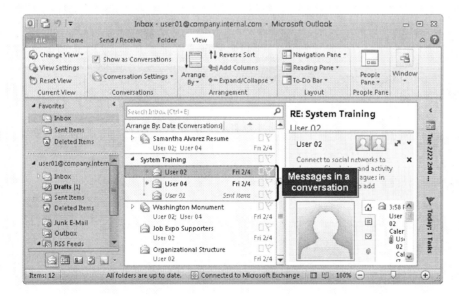

Figure 6-2: *Email conversations in the Inbox.*

The Conversation view can be customized by using the **Conversation Settings** option in the **Arrangement** group of the **View** tab.

Option	Description
Show Messages from Other Folders	This is the default option that allows you to display related messages from other folders such as Sent Items. You can view the message from other folders without having to leave the Inbox.
Show Senders above the Subject	This option displays the name of the sender above the subject. It is useful for locating messages based on senders.
Always Expand Conversations	This option allows you to view all the messages in a conversation. By default, only the latest messages in the conversation are displayed.
Use Classic Indented View	This view indents the older messages in a conversation and arranges them in the Inbox.

The Move Tool

The **Move** tool is present in the **Move** group of the **Home** tab and helps you organize conversations by moving them into specific folders. You can also choose the **Always Move Messages in This Conversation** option to move new messages in a conversation to a specific folder in Outlook.

The Ignore Command

The **Ignore** command provides options to ignore messages in a conversation and move them to the **Deleted Items** folder. When you ignore a conversation thread, all future messages relating to that conversation are ignored. You can recover the messages of conversation that are ignored by selecting the ignored message from the **Deleted Items** folder and selecting the **Stop Ignoring** option of the **Ignore** command.

The Clean Up Command

The **Clean Up** command, available in the **Delete** group of the **Home** tab, allows you to move redundant messages of a conversation. By default, messages that are cleaned up are sent to the **Deleted Items** folder. You can also specify to move the cleaned-up messages into a folder of your choice. The options to clean up a specified set of messages and folders, and the location to which the cleaned-up items will be moved, can be set in the **Outlook Options** dialog box.

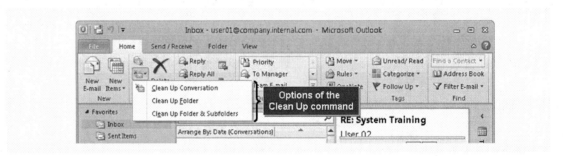

Figure 6-3: The Clean Up command options.

 When you use the **Clean Up** command for the first time, the **Clean Up Conversation** message box is displayed.

The **Clean Up** command provides three options.

Clean Up Command	Description
Clean Up Conversation	Deletes redundant messages in a conversation.
Clean Up Folder	Moves redundant messages from the current folder to the **Deleted Items** folder.
Clean Up Folders & Subfolders	Moves redundant messages from the current folder, as well as its subfolders, to the **Deleted Items** folder.

Redundant Messages

When you delete a conversation, only those messages that are already a part of the latest email in the conversation are deleted. The latest email displaying the conversation is retained.

How to Manage Email Messages

Procedure Reference: Format Text Using the Mini Toolbar

To format text using the Mini toolbar:

1. If necessary, create a new email message and enter text in the body of the message.
2. Select the text that needs to be formatted.
3. Apply the desired formatting changes using the Mini toolbar.
   - From the **Font** drop-down list, select the desired font.
   - From the **Font Size** drop-down list, select the desired font size.
   - Click the **Grow Font** or **Shrink Font** button to increase or decrease the font size.
   - Click the **Decrease Indent** or **Increase Indent** button to decrease or increase indent.
   - Click the **Bold, Italic,** or **Underline** button to bold face, italicize, or underline text.
   - Click the **Center** button to center the text.
   - Select the **Font Color** and **Text Highlight Color** options to change the color of the font or to highlight it.

Procedure Reference: Flag an Email Message for Follow-Up

To flag an email message for follow-up:

1. Display the **Follow Up** options.
   - In the Inbox, right-click the message that needs to be flagged and from the displayed menu, choose **Follow Up** or;
   - In the Inbox, select the message, and on the **Home** tab, in the **Tags** group, click **Follow Up** or;
   - In the Inbox, open the message that needs to be flagged, and on the **Message** tab, in the **Tags** group, click **Follow Up.**
2. Select an option from the **Follow Up** options to add a flag.

 When a flagged message is due to be followed up, the text in the message header will change from black to red.

3. If necessary, view the flagged message in the **For Follow Up** folder.

    a. On the **Folder** tab, in the **New** group, click **New Search Folder.**

    b. In the **New Search Folder** dialog box, in the **Select a Search Folder** list box, select **Mail flagged for follow up** and click **OK.**

    c. In the Navigation pane, click **Search Folders** to view the **For Follow Up** folder with the flagged messages.

Procedure Reference: Add a Reminder to an Email Message for Follow-Up

To add a reminder to an email message for follow-up:

1. Select the email message that needs to be flagged.

2. Display the **Custom** dialog box.

- On the **Home** tab, in the **Tags** group, click **Follow Up,** and from the displayed menu, click **Add Reminder** or;

- Right-click the message and from the displayed menu, choose **Follow Up→Custom.**

 When the **Add Reminder** option is selected, the **Reminder** option is set by default. The **Reminder** option needs to be manually set only when the **Custom** option is selected.

3. In the **Custom** dialog box, set the required flagging options.

- From the **Flag to** drop-down list, select the desired option.

- Click the **Start date** drop-down arrow and select a start date from the calendar.

- Click the **Due date** drop-down arrow and select an end date from the calendar.

- If necessary, check the **Reminder** check box, and from the drop-down list, select the desired date, time, and sound alerts.

- If necessary, click **Clear Flag** to clear the flag options that were set in the **Custom** dialog box.

4. Click **OK** to close the **Custom** dialog box.

5. If necessary, in the Navigation pane, click **Search Folders** to view the **For Follow Up** folder with the flagged messages.

Procedure Reference: Create a Quick Step

To create a quick step:

1. If necessary, switch to the Mail view.

2. On the **Home** tab, in the **Quick Steps** group, click **Create New.**

3. In the **Actions** section, select the actions for the quick step.

- From the **Choose an Action** drop-down list, select an action or;

- Click **Add Action,** and from the **Choose an Action** drop-down list, select an action to add an additional action.

4. In the **Name** text box, enter a name for the new quick step.

5. If necessary, click the icon to the left of the **Name** text box, and in the **Choose an icon** dialog box, click an icon and click **OK** to change the icon for the new quick step.

ACTIVITY 6-1
Managing Email Messages

Scenario:

You received an email message from a client with the product list of gourmet beans and would like to follow up with the client about the products. You want to mark the email message and set a reminder so that you can follow up with her about it. You want to create a folder where you can refer to important email messages. Moreover, you find that your mailbox is filled with messages that you no longer need. You decide to organize your email by cleaning up your email account.

---

1. Flag the Product List email message with a reminder.

    a. Launch the Microsoft Outlook 2010 application.

    b. In the Inbox, in the View pane, select the **Product List** message.

    c. On the **Home** tab, in the **Tags** group, from the **Follow Up** drop-down list, select **Add Reminder.**

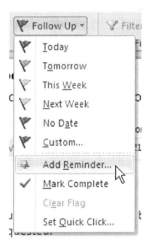

    d. In the **Custom** dialog box, click the **Due date** drop-down arrow, and in the calendar that is displayed, select the next business day.

    e. In the **Reminder** section, in the Time drop-down list, scroll up, select **10:00 AM** and click **OK.**

    f. In the View pane, observe that the message is flagged, and the alarm icon is displayed.

---

2. Display the contents of the **For Follow Up** folder.

a. Select the **Folder** tab, and in the **New** group, click **New Search Folder.**

b. In the **New Search Folder** dialog box, in the **Reading Mail** section, select the **Mail flagged for follow up** option and click **OK.**

c. Observe that the Product List message is displayed in the **For Follow Up** folder.

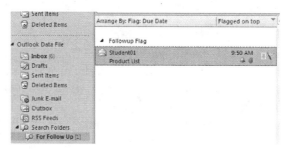

d. In the Navigation pane, click **Inbox.**

3. Create a folder for priority email messages.

a. On the **Folder** tab, in the **New** group, click **New Folder.**

b. In the **Create New Folder** dialog box, in the **Name** text box, type *Priority*

c. In the **Select where to place the folder** list box, verify that **Inbox** is selected and click **OK.**

d. In the Navigation pane, observe that the Priority subfolder is added below Inbox.

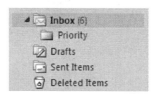

e. Select the **Home** tab, and in the **Quick Steps** group, click the **More** button, and then from the displayed list, select **Create New.**

f. In the **Edit Quick Step** dialog box, in the **Actions** section, from the **Choose an Action** drop-down list, in the **Filing** section, select **Move to folder.**

g. From **Choose folder** drop-down list, select **Priority** and click **Finish.**

h. In the View pane, verify that the Product List message is selected, and on the **Home** tab, in the **Quick Steps** group, click **Priority.**

i. In the Navigation pane, click the **Priority** folder.

j. Observe that the Product List email is moved to the folder.

k. In the Navigation pane, click **Inbox** to view the email in the Inbox.

4. Organize email according to conversations.

a. Select the **View** tab, and in the **Conversations** group, check the **Show as Conversations** check box.

b. In the **Microsoft Outlook** alert box, select **This Folder.**

c.   Observe that the Lunch messages in the Inbox are grouped as a conversation.

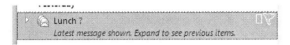

5.   Clean up a conversation.

a.   In the View pane, select the **Lunch** conversation that you want to clean up.

b.   Select the **Home** tab and in the **Delete** group, from the **Clean Up** drop-down list, select **Clean Up Conversation.**

c.   In the **Clean Up Conversation** message box, click **Clean Up** to move redundant messages to the **Deleted Items** folder and in the **Microsoft Outlook** message box, click **OK.**

d.   Observe that the number of messages in the conversation is reduced.

e.   In the Navigation pane, click **Deleted Items.**

f.   Observe that the deleted email of the conversation is present in this folder.

6.   Ignore future messages in the conversation.

a.   In the Navigation pane, select **Inbox.**

b.   On the **Home** tab, in the **Delete** group, click **Ignore.**

c.   In the **Ignore Conversation** message box, click **Ignore Conversation** to move the selected conversation and future messages to the **Deleted Items** folder.

d.   Select the **Deleted Items** folder.

e.   Double-click the third **Lunch** message, and in the message form, in the **Respond** group, click **Reply.**

f.   In the message form, in the **To** text box, type your partner's address and click **Send.**

g.   Close the Lunch message form.

h.   In the Navigation pane, select **Inbox.**

i.   Observe that you have not received the message from this conversation that was sent by your partner.

j.   In the Navigation pane, click **Deleted Items.**

k.   Observe that the ignored message from this conversation sent by your partner is displayed.

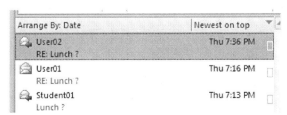

l.   In the Navigation pane, click **Inbox.**

m.   Select the **View** tab, and in the **Conversations** group, uncheck the **Show as Conversations** check box.

n.   In the **Microsoft Outlook** message box, click **This folder.**

TOPIC B
Locate Information Quickly

You managed some of your email messages. Now, you are ready to search for messages that contain a specific piece of text or satisfy multiple criteria and quickly view necessary messages. In this topic, you will locate information efficiently.

In the course of your work, at times, you may have to refer to older email messages. Imagine you have multiple folders in Outlook and have stored hundreds of email in each of these folders. This makes it difficult to find an email message when needed. Outlook's Instant Search feature makes locating items that contain specific text quick and easy.

The Instant Search Feature

Outlook's *Instant Search* feature allows you to quickly search for items by specifying search criteria. It enables you to search in different views using the **Instant Search** pane and specify different search options. It also allows you to modify different search criteria to suit your requirements. This feature works by indexing items and then accessing the indexed items as needed. The **Instant Search** pane is available in different views such as **Mail, Calendar, Contacts, Tasks, Notes, Folder List,** and **Journal.**

Figure 6-4: The Instant Search pane in the Mail view.

When searching for items, Outlook displays the **Search Tools** contextual tab that provides additional search options. You can change search options by clicking **Search Tools** in the **Options** group of the **Search Tools** contextual tab and then selecting the **Search Options.** This option displays the **Search** tab in the **Outlook Options** dialog box, where you can specify the required options.

The Advanced Find Dialog Box

The **Advanced Find** dialog box is used to locate items by using specific criteria to narrow down a search. This is a contextual feature with a default [Outlook item] tab that is displayed based on the current view in Outlook.

Option	Allows You To
The **Look for** drop-down list	Select the types of Outlook items to search for, such as messages, tasks, notes, appointments, meetings, and contacts.
The **Browse** button	Specify the folder in which the search needs to be performed.
The default [Outlook item] tab	Enter the details of the selected item, depending upon the current view that is selected. The options displayed on this tab depend on the choice that is made in the **Look for** text box.
The **More Choices** tab	Categorize email messages, based on the read or unread status, attachments, the priority level, color categories, the flagged status, and size.
The **Advanced** tab	Define the criteria based on different fields, conditions, or specific values.
The **Find Now** button	Look for a particular word or phrase that is specified in the **Search for the word(s)** text box.
The **New Search** button	Clear the current search and perform a new search.

How to Locate Information Quickly

Procedure Reference: Search for Items in Outlook

To search for items in Outlook:

1. Select the folders that are to be searched.

2. In the **Instant Search** text box, enter the search text.

3. On the **Search Tools** contextual tab, in the **Scope** group, choose the required command.

   - Click **All Mail Items** to search the email items in all the folders.

   - Click **Current Folder** to search within the current folder.

   - Click **All Outlook Items** to search all the items.

4. On the **Search Tools** contextual tab, in the **Refine** group, select the required option.

   - Click **From** to search for messages from a particular sender.

   - Click **Subject** to search for messages with a particular subject.

   - Click **Has Attachments** to search for messages that contain attachments.

   - Click **Categorized,** and from the displayed menu, choose an option to search by category.

     - Select **Any Category** to search for messages from any category.

     - Select **No Categories** to search for messages that are not categorized.

   - Click **This Week,** and from the displayed menu, choose an option to search the message by date.

   - Click **Sent To,** and from the displayed menu, choose an option to search by sender.

- ■ Select **Sent To: Me or CC: Me** to search for messages that were sent directly to you or in which you were on the CC list.

- ■ Select **Not Sent Directly to Me** to search for messages that were not sent directly to you.

- ■ Select **Sent to Another Recipient** to search for messages that were sent to another recipient.

- Click **Unread** to display the unread messages that match the search criteria.

- Click **Flagged** to display the flagged messages that match the search criteria.

- Click **Important** to display messages that have a specific priority level and match the search criteria.

- Click **More,** and from the displayed menu, choose an option to display messages with the chosen field, and match the search criteria.

5. On the **Search Tools** contextual tab, in the **Options** group, select the required search option.

- Click **Recent Searches** and select a recent search to repeat the search.

- Click **Search Tools** and select an option to use advanced search tools.

- ■ Click **Indexing Status** to check the number of items remaining that need to be indexed.

- ■ Click **Locations to Search** and choose an email account.

- ■ Click **Advanced Find** to perform a search by using advanced search criteria.

- ■ Click **Search Options** to specify or modify the search options in the **Outlook Options** dialog box.

6. If necessary, in the **Close** group of the **Search Tools** contextual tab, click **Close Search** to close the current search.

Procedure Reference: Search for Items Using Multiple Criteria

To search for items using multiple criteria:

1. On the **Search Tools** contextual tab, in the **Options** group, click **Advanced Find.**

2. From the **Look for** drop-down list, select the item that you want to search for.

3. In the **Search for the word(s)** text box, type the search terms.

4. If necessary, click **Browse,** and in the **Select Folder(s)** dialog box, select the folder to be searched, and click **OK** to display the appropriate folder in the **In** text box.

5. In the **From** text box, specify a person's name whose email you need to search for.

6. Click **Find Now** to display the items that match the criteria in the **Advanced Find** dialog box.

7. If necessary, select the **More Choices** tab and select the required options.

- Click **Categories,** and from the **Color Categories** drop-down list, select a color category to filter the search results based on the color category.

- Check the **Only items that are** check box to search for read or unread messages.

- Check the **Only items with** check box to search for messages with attachments.

- Check the **Whose importance is** check box to search for messages with a normal, low, or high priority.

- Check the **Only items which** check box to search for messages that are flagged or completed.

- From the **Size** drop-down list, select an option to specify the size of the message.

8. If necessary, select the **Advanced** tab and select the required options.

   a. In the **Define more criteria** section, from the **Field** drop-down list, select a particular field and specify conditions and values.

   b. Click **Add to List** to add criteria to the **Find items that match this criteria** list box.

9. Click **Find Now** to search with the specified criteria.

ACTIVITY 6-2
Searching for an Email Message

Scenario:
You received several email messages from your client with the product list for the gourmet beans, which their company, Everything for Coffee, manufactures. Because you have not yet responded to the message, you decide to search for the message so that you can follow up on it. You also want to specify advanced search options to customize the search.

1. Search for the email message with the word "Job."

    a. In the Inbox, above the View pane, click the **Search Inbox** text box.

    b. Observe that the **Search Tools** contextual tab is displayed on the Ribbon.

    c. In the **Search Inbox** text box, type **J**

    d. Observe that relevant search results are displayed as you type the text.

    e. Type **ob**

    f. Observe that the email messages that contain the word "Job" are displayed in the search results and the matching words in the email are highlighted in yellow.

    g. Click the **Close Search** button to close the search box. ⓧ

    h. In the Inbox, above the View pane, click the **Search Inbox** text box.

2. Search for an email based on specific criteria.

    a. On the **Search Tools** contextual tab, in the **Refine** group, click **Important.**

    b. Observe that the email that is marked as important is displayed.

    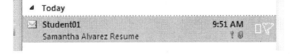

TOPIC C
Share Calendar Information

You worked with email messages. When collaborating with others, you may want to share information about your schedule with them. In this topic, you will share your calendar information.

There may be situations where you want to share your calendar information with your team. In some cases, the team may be spread across different locations or use different applications to manage their schedules. Outlook 2010 allows you to share your calendar by using email, to set permission to access your calender for your delegates, and to publish the calendar to Office Online.

The To-Do Bar

The *To-Do Bar* is used to manage daily tasks and appointments. The To-Do Bar contains three sections: the Date Navigator that displays the current month, a list that displays appointments and meetings, and a list of tasks and to-do items. The To-Do Bar can be customized to display only the information that you require.

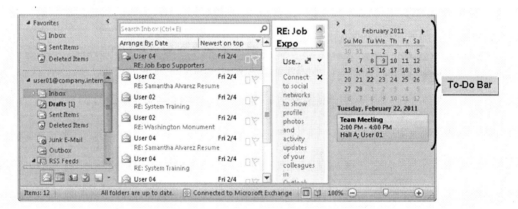

Figure 6-5: *The To-Do Bar displaying a calendar and appointments.*

The Schedule View

The *Schedule* view allows you to view multiple calendars in a horizontal layout, and to compare and modify schedules. This view is useful when you select multiple calendars to check and to schedule appointments or meetings. You can automatically view calendars either in the Vertical or Schedule layout, depending on the number of calendars set using the **Calendar** tab of the **Outlook Options** dialog box. The option to display the calendar in the Schedule View is available in the **Arrange** group of the **Home** tab.

The Send a Calendar via E-mail Dialog Box

The *Send a Calendar via E-mail* dialog box allows you to send calendars to other users through an email message. You can access this dialog box by selecting the **E-mail Calendar** option in the **Share** group of the **Home** tab in the Calendar view.

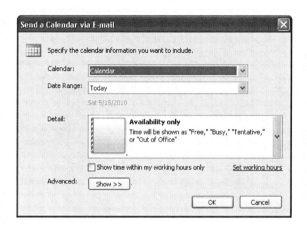

Figure 6-6: *The options in the Send a Calendar via E-mail dialog box.*

The options in the **Send a Calendar via E-mail** dialog box allow you to set the date range, working hours, time availability, and the free/busy information that you want to share.

Option	Enables You To
Calendar	Choose a calendar to send from a list of available calendars.
Date Range	Specify a date range you want to send.
Detail	Set the level of detail to be sent with the calendar. The options are: • **Availability only:** Shows the availability status as free, busy, or out of the office. • **Limited details:** Limits details to availability and subject of calendar items. • **Full details:** Shows the availability and full details of calendar items.
Show time within my working hours only	Specify your working hours, add holidays, propose new meeting times, and display options and time zones.
Advanced	Include items marked private, attach files, and set email layouts.

Calendar Groups

A *calendar group* allows you to view multiple calendars of other users together to compare their schedules before you schedule a meeting. The **Calendar Groups** command can be accessed from the **Manage Calendars** group of the **Home** tab. You can either create a new calendar group using the **Create New Calendar Group** command, or create a group of calendars to be displayed using the **Save as New Calendar Group** command. Calendar groups are listed in the Navigation pane of the Calendar view.

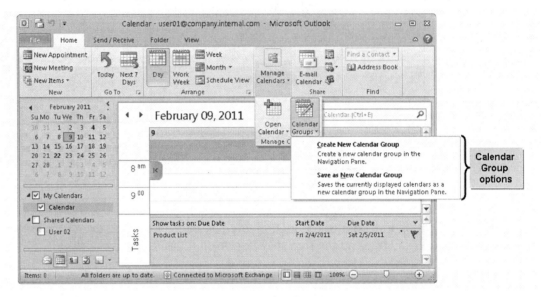

Figure 6-7: Options to create or save a new calendar group.

Calendar Overlays

Outlook provides you with the option of viewing multiple calendars at the same time. To view multiple calendars, use the Overlay mode to stack calendars one on top of the other. You can access the **Overlay** option by right-clicking the calendar and choosing **Overlay.** The Overlay mode can be used to stack default Outlook calendars, shared calendars from other people, Internet calendars, or Internet calendar subscriptions. This mode is useful for finding the free/busy information of other people and viewing any meeting requests they accepted.

Delegates

A delegate is a person who is given permission to access another user's Outlook folders. You can add users and grant them permission to send and modify items using the **Delegate Access** option available in the **Account Setting** drop-down list. Once a delegate is added, you can set the required permission levels. Permission levels include enabling delegates to author or review items in the various Outlook folders.

Internet Calendar Subscriptions

You can subscribe to and download a calendar from a calendar publishing service or a website and view it in Outlook. Using this calendar, you can exchange calendar information with other Outlook users regardless of the application that is used to create or view the information. All Internet calendars use the iCalendar format with the .ics file extension. Once a calendar is downloaded and executed, it gets added to the Navigation pane in the Calendar view in the **Other Calendars** section and opens side-by-side along with the default Outlook calendar. The downloaded calendar checks for periodic updates made by the calendar publisher and automatically updates when an update is available. The websites that allow you to download calendars begin with the **webcal://** protocol.

Publishing Calendars Online

In Outlook, you can publish your Internet calendar to Office Online. This enables you to share your calendar with multiple users or designated users.

How to Share Calendar Information

Procedure Reference: Send Calendar Information Through Email

To send calendar information through email:

1. If necessary, switch to the Calendar view.
2. On the **Home** tab, in the **Share** group, click **E-mail Calendar** to display the **Send a Calendar via E-mail** dialog box.
3. Specify the calendar information you want to include.
   a. In the **Send a Calendar via E-mail** dialog box, from the **Calendar** drop-down list, verify that **Calendar** is selected.
   b. From the **Date Range** drop-down list, select the desired date range to specify the calendar information for the selected date range.
   c. From the **Detail** drop-down list, select the desired option to specify the available details of calendar items.
4. Click **OK** to close the **Send a Calendar via E-mail** dialog box and to attach the calendar information in the message body.
5. In the message body, in the **To** text box, type the name of the recipient who will receive the calendar.
6. Click **Send** to send the calendar information to the recipient.

Procedure Reference: Share a Calendar

To share a calendar:

1. On the **Home** tab, in the **Share** group, click the **Share Calendar** button.
2. In the Sharing Invitation Message form, in the **To** text box, type the name of a contact with whom you want to share the calendar.
3. Send the message.
4. In the **Microsoft Outlook** dialog box that asks for confirmation, click **Yes** to share the calendar.

Procedure Reference: View a Shared Calendar

To view a shared calendar:

1. Open the desired Sharing Invitation Message form.

2. In the Sharing Invitation Message form, on the **Share** tab, in the **Open** group, click **Open this Calendar** to view your default calendar and your partner's calendar side-by-side.

Procedure Reference: View Calendars in the Overlay Mode

To view calendars in the Overlay mode:

1. In the Navigation pane, in the **All Calendar Items** section, right-click the other user's name and choose **Overlay** to view the calendar in the Overlay mode.

2. If necessary, right-click the other user's name and choose **Overlay** again to switch back to the default calendar view.

Procedure Reference: Delegate Access to Folders

To delegate access to folders:

1. On the **File** tab, choose **Info.**

2. In the Backstage view, in the **Account Information** section, from the **Account Settings** drop-down list, select **Delegate Access.**

3. In the **Delegates** dialog box, click **Add.**

4. In the **Add Users** dialog box, select the person you want as a delegate and click **OK.**

5. In the **Delegate Permissions** dialog box, from the **Calendar** drop-down list, select an option to set the permission levels for your calendar folder.

    *   Select **Editor (can read, create, and modify items)** to allow the delegate to read, create, and modify items on your calendar.

    *   Select **Author (can read and create items)** to allow the delegate to read and create items on your calendar.

    *   Select **Reviewer (can read items)** to allow the delegate to only review items on your calendar.

    *   Select **None** to deny the delegate to access your calendar folder.

6. Similarly, select an option each from the **Tasks, Inbox, Contacts, Notes,** and **Journal** drop-down lists and click **OK.**

7. In the **Delegates** dialog box, set options to decide on the delivery of responses for meeting requests you organized.

    *   Select the **My delegates only, but send a copy of meeting requests and responses to me (recommended)** option to send responses to the delegates and a copy to the organizer.

    *   Select the **My delegates only** option to send the response only to the delegates.

    *   Select the **My delegates and me** option to send the response both to the delegates and the organizer.

8. Click **OK** to close the dialog box.

Procedure Reference: Publish Calendar Information to Office Online

To publish calendar information to Office Online:

1. Display the calendar you want to publish.

2. In the Navigation pane, in the **Calendar** section, right-click **Calendar** and choose **Share→Publish to Office.com.**

3. In the **Office.com Registration** wizard, click **Sign in.**

4. On the **Microsoft Outlook Calendar Sharing Service** page, in the **E-mail address** text box, type your Windows Live ID.

5. In the **Password** text box, type your password.

6. Click **Sign in** to sign in to the Office Online service.

7. On the **Sign In Complete** page, click **Finish.**

8. In the **Publish Calendar to Office.com** dialog box, in the **Permissions** section, select an option.

    ● Select **Only invited users can view this calendar** to allow only invited users to view the calendar.

    ● Select **Anyone can subscribe to this calendar** to allow all users to view the calendar.

9. Click **OK** to publish the calendar.

10. Specify whether to send the sharing invitation to other users.

    ● In the **Send a Sharing Invitation** dialog box, click **Yes** to send the invitation.

    ● In the **Send a Sharing Invitation** dialog box, click **No** to prevent the invitation from being sent.

11. In the Internet Calendar - Share Message form, in the **To** text box, type the user name to whom you want to send the invitation.

12. Send the invitation.

Procedure Reference: Display and Customize the To Do Bar

To display and customize the To Do Bar:

1. On the **View** tab, in the **Layout** group, click the **To-Do Bar** drop-down arrow.

    ● Click **Normal** to display the To Do Bar in the Normal view.

    ● Click **Minimized** to minimize the To Do Bar.

    ● Click **Off** to hide the To-Do Bar.

2. Check or uncheck the **Date Navigator** check box to display or hide the calendar date navigator.

3. Check or uncheck the **Appointments** check box to display or hide appointments.

4. Check or uncheck the **Checklist** check box to display or hide the checklist.

ACTIVITY 6-3
Scheduling a Meeting and Sending Calendar Information in an Email Message

Scenario:
You want to schedule a team meeting with your colleagues. A colleague has asked you to send him your calendar information for the next 30 days. He says that he wants to view the details of your schedule. You decide to send him your schedule details in an email message.

---

1. Schedule a meeting.

    a. In the Navigation pane, click **Calendar.**

    b. On the **Home** tab, in the **Arrange** group, click **Schedule View.**

    c. In the **New** group, click **New Meeting.**

    d. In the Meeting form, in the **To** text box, type the email address of your partner.

    e. In the Meeting form, in the **Subject** text box, type *Team Meeting* and press **Tab.**

    f. Click **Rooms.**

    g. In the **Select Rooms : All Rooms** dialog box, verify that Conference Room A is selected, click **Rooms,** and then click **OK.**

    h. In the **Show** group, click **Scheduling Assistant,** and in the displayed **Room Finder** task pane, select the next business day.

    i. In the **All Attendees** column, hover the mouse pointer over each attendee to check whether they are free for the meeting.

    j. Beside the **Attendees** column, click the **10.00** column.

    k. In the **End Time** text box, click the time drop-down arrow and select **11.00 AM (1 hour)** and then click **Send.**

---

2. Specify the calendar information you want to include.

    a. On the **Home** tab, in the **Share** group, click **E-mail Calendar.**

    b. In the **Send a Calendar via E-mail** dialog box, in the **Calendar** drop-down list, verify that **Calendar** is selected.

    c. From the **Date Range** drop-down list, select **Next 30 days.**

d.   From the **Detail** drop-down list, select **Full details** and click **OK.**

e.   In the Message form, observe that the calendar is attached to the message body.

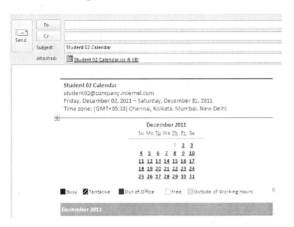

3.   Send the calendar information.

a.   In the Message form, in the **To** text box, click and type your partner's name.

b.   Click **Send** to send the calendar information.

c.   Switch to the Mail view and in the View pane, click the calendar sent by your partner.

4.   Send an invitation to share your calendar.

a.   Switch to the Calendar view.

b.   On the **Home** tab, in the **Share** group, click **Share Calendar.**

c.   In the Message form, in the **To** text box, type your partner's name.

d.   From the **Details** drop-down list, select **Full details** and click **Send.**

e.   In the **Microsoft Outlook** message box, click **Yes** to share the Calendar.

5.   View the shared calendar in the Overlay mode.

a.   Display the Inbox.

b.   Open the Sharing Invitation Message form sent by your partner..

c.   In the Sharing Invitation Message form, in the **Open** group, click **Open this Calendar.**

d.   If necessary, maximize the Outlook window.

e.   In the **Arrange** group, click **Day.**

f.   Observe that the Calendar view displays your partner's calendar and your calendar side-by-side.

g. In the Navigation pane, in the **Calendar** section, right-click your partner's calendar, and from the displayed menu, choose **Overlay.**

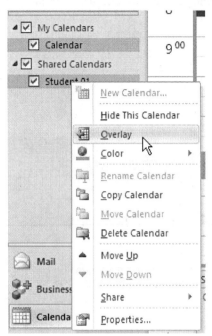

h. Observe that the calendars are displayed in Overlay mode.

i. In the **Calendar** section, right-click your partner's calendar, and from the displayed menu, choose **Overlay** again to remove the calendars from the Overlay mode.

ACTIVITY 6-4
Publishing the Calendar to Microsoft Office Online

Before You Begin:

Switch to the Calendar view and display just your calendar.

Scenario:

You are the captain of the soccer team at your company. You regularly update your calendar information with the practice schedule and game dates. Because you may need to update your calendar after office hours, you decide to publish your calendar to Office Online and invite all your team members to view the calendar. This allows your team, as well as others attending the game, to view the updated game timelines from Office Online.

1. Register with Office Online to publish the calendar.

    a. In the Calendar view, select your calendar.

    b. On the **Home** tab, in the **Share** group, from the **Publish Online** drop-down list, select **Publish to Office.com.**

    c. In the **Security** alert box, click **OK.**

    d. In the **Office.com Registration** wizard, on the **Microsoft Outlook Calendar Sharing Service** page, click **Sign in.**

    e. On the **Microsoft Office Online Registration** page, in the **E-mail address** text box, type your Windows Live ID.

    f. In the **Password** text box, type the password and click **Sign in** to sign in to the Office Online service.

    g. On the **Sign In Complete** page, click **Finish.**

2. Apply calendar sharing settings.

    a. In the **Publish Calendar to Office.com** dialog box, in the **Permissions** section, select the **Anyone can subscribe to this calendar** option and click **OK.**

    b. In the **Send a Sharing Invitation** alert boxbox, click **Yes.**

    c. In the Message form, in the **To** text box, type the desired user name and click **Send** to send the share invitation to the user.

3. View the calendar that is published to Office Online.

    a. In the Mail view, in the View pane, double-click and open the calendar message from your partner.

    b. In the **[User name]_Calendar - Internet Calendar - Share** message, on the **Share** tab, in the **Open** group, click **Subscribe to this Calendar.**

    c. In the **Microsoft Outlook** dialog box, click **Yes** to add this calendar to Outlook and subscribe to updates.

d. In the Navigation pane, observe that your partner's Internet calendar is displayed in the **Shared Calendars** section.

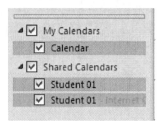

TOPIC D
Share Contact Information

You are familiar with creating contacts. Outlook provides you with the option of sending contact information to another recipient through email. In this topic, you will share information using an electronic business card.

There may be times when someone will ask you to send them information on one of your contacts. Instead of writing down all the details in an email, you can attach the contact's information in an email and send it. It is also better if the recipient can view the contact information in a format similar to the paper-based business card format. Outlook makes the task easier by allowing recipients to save the contact as a contact record.

Search Contacts

The **Find a Contact** text box in the **Find** group on the **Home** tab allows you to find contacts from your address book. You can find contacts from within the Mail view itself. The search result displays not only the contact window for the searched contact, but also different ways of communicating with the contact.

Electronic Business Cards

An *Electronic Business Card (EBC)* is the electronic version of a business card that displays contact details. It is automatically created when you create a contact entry in Outlook. The contact details displayed include the name of the contact, employer, designation, phone numbers, and email address. Other contact information specified in the contact entry can also be displayed, and can include an image of the contact. The background and layout of an EBC can be modified to suit individual preferences. You can insert an EBC of a contact in an email message to share the contact details with others, or include an EBC in your email signature.

Figure 6-8: *Display of an electronic business card.*

The Edit Business Card Dialog Box

The **Edit Business Card** dialog box enables you to format the appearance of electronic business cards and the contact information displayed in them.

Section	Description
Fields	Lists fields that are added as contact information in a business card. New fields can be added to the business card, and existing fields can be edited or deleted.
Card Design	Allows you to modify the design of a card. An image can be added by clicking **Change** and then choosing an image in the **Add Card Picture** dialog box. The card can then be customized by changing the layout, alignment, background color, and area of the image.
Edit	Displays text in the format appropriate for the field selected in the **Fields** section. The text and labels for the field can then be customized by selecting an option from the different formatting options provided in the **Edit** section for the text.
Preview	Shows a preview of a business card. Any changes made to a business card are reflected here.

How to Share Contact Information

Procedure Reference: Edit a Business Card

To edit a business card:

1. In the Contacts view, open a contact.
2. Display the **Edit Business Card** dialog box.
   - In the Contact form, on the **Contact** tab, in the **Options** group, click **Business Card.**
   - In the Contact form, double-click the business card or;
   - In the Contact form, right-click the business card and choose **Edit Business Card.**
3. In the **Edit Business Card** dialog box, in the **Fields** list box, select the desired field.
4. If necessary, below the **Fields** list box, click **Add,** and from the displayed menu, choose a category. From the submenu, choose the field that you want to add to the list box.
5. In the **Edit** section, in the text box, type the information for the corresponding field that is added.
6. If necessary, from the **Label** drop-down list, select an option to specify the location of the label.
   - Select **Left** to display the label on the left side of the business card.
   - Select **Right** to display the label on the right side of the business card.
7. If necessary, in the **Label** text box, type a name for the label.
8. If necessary, remove a field from the business card.
   a. In the **Fields** list box, select the field that needs to be removed.
   b. Click **Remove** to remove the selected field.
9. Click **OK** to save the business card.

Procedure Reference: Format the Appearance of a Business Card

To format the appearance of a business card:

1. In the Contacts view, open a contact.
2. On the **Contact** tab, in the **Options** group, click **Business Card.**
3. In the **Edit Business Card** dialog box, in the **Card Design** section, specify the settings to format the business card.

    ● From the **Layout** drop-down list, select an option to specify the location of the image.

      ■ Select **Image Left** to place the image to the left of the business card.

      ■ Select **Image Right** to place the image to the right of the business card.

      ■ Select **Image Top** to place the image at the top of the business card.

      ■ Select **Image Bottom** to place the image at the bottom of the business card.

      ■ Select **Text Only** to display only text on the business card.

      ■ Select **Background Image** to display the image as the background image.

    ● Set a background color for the business card.

      a. Click the **Background Color** button.

      b. In the **Color** dialog box, from the displayed palette, select a color.

      c. If necessary, define a color.

        A. Click **Define Custom Colors** to display the rainbow color palette.

        B. Select a color, and click **Add to Custom Colors** to add the selected color to the **Custom Colors** section.

      d. Click **OK.**

    ● Insert an image in the business card.

      a. From the **Image** drop-down list, select **Change.**

      b. In the **Add Card Picture** dialog box, select an image.

      c. Click **OK** to insert the selected image in the business card.

    ● In the **Image Area** spin box, click the up or down arrow to set the size of the image.

    ● From the **Image Align** drop-down list, select an option to align the image in the business card.

4. In the **Edit Business Card** dialog box, in the **Fields** list box, select a field so that the corresponding text for the field is displayed in the **Edit** text box.

5. In the **Edit Business Card** dialog box, in the **Edit** section, format the text displayed in the **Edit** text box.

 Format text options include increasing or decreasing font size, adding bold or italic formatting, underlining text, and changing font color. You can also change the color of the label.

6. In the **Edit Business Card** dialog box, click **OK** to apply formatting to the business card.

7. Save and close the contact.

Procedure Reference: Create an E-mail Signature

To create an e-mail signature:

1. On the **File** tab, choose **Options.**

2. In the **Outlook Options** dialog box, select the **Mail** category, and in the **Compose Messages** section, click **Signatures** to display the **Signatures and Stationery** dialog box.

3. In the **Signatures and Stationery** dialog box, on the **E-mail Signature** tab, below the **Select signature to edit** list box, click **New** to display the **New Signature** dialog box.

4. In the **New Signature** dialog box, in the **Type a name for this signature** text box, type a name and click **OK** to create a new signature.

5. In the **Edit signature** section, in the text area, type the text for the signature.

6. If necessary, change the font, font size, and font color of the signature text.

   a. In the **Edit signature** section, in the text area, select the signature text that you entered.

   b. From the **Font** drop-down list, select a font.

   c. From the **Font Size** drop-down list, select a font size.

   d. From the **Font Color** drop-down list, select a font color.

7. If necessary, include a business card in the signature.

   a. In the **Edit signature** section, in the text box, click where you want the card to be displayed.

   b. In the **Edit signature** section, click **Business Card.**

   c. In the **Insert Business Card** dialog box, in the **Filed As** list box, select a contact and click **OK.**

8. If necessary, include a picture in the signature.

   a. In the **Edit signature** section, in the text box, click where you want the picture to be displayed.

   b. Click the **Picture** button.

   c. In the **Insert Picture** dialog box, select an image and click **Insert.**

9. If necessary, include a hyperlink in the signature.

   a. In the **Edit signature** section, in the text box, click where you want the link to be displayed.

   b. Click the **Insert Hyperlink** button.

   c. In the **Insert Hyperlink** dialog box, select the hyperlink, or type an address, and click **OK.**

10. In the **Signatures and Stationery** dialog box, in the **Choose default signature** section, from the **New messages** drop-down list, select **(none)** to prevent the signature from being automatically inserted in the messages that you send.

 By default, **(none)** is displayed in the **New messages** drop-down list. You need to explicitly select the option again to prevent the insertion of the signature in all the messages.

11. If necessary, from the **Replies/forwards** drop-down list, select a signature to include in the messages that you forward or reply to, or select **(none)** to prevent a signature from being automatically inserted when you are replying or forwarding messages.

12. Click **OK** to apply the changes and close the **Signatures and Stationery** dialog box.

13. Click **OK** to close the **Outlook Options** dialog box.

Procedure Reference: Send a Business Card in an Email Message

To send a business card in an email message:

1. Open a new Message form.

2. In the **To, Cc,** and **Subject** fields, enter the required information.

3. Click the body of the message, select the **Insert** tab, and in the **Include** group, click **Business Card.** From the displayed list, select a business card to insert it in the message.

4. Send the email.

ACTIVITY 6-5
Editing a Business Card

Data Files:

C\084574Data\Managing Information at Work\Angela.jpg

Scenario:

You receive a mail from a colleague with her Business Card as her signature. You want to learn how to include your Business Card in your email. Your colleague has agreed to show you how to insert and format a Business Card in your email.

---

1. Add the IM address and home phone number to the business card.

    a. Switch to the Contacts view and double-click the **Angela Barry** contact.

    b. In the **Internet** section, in the **IM address** text box, click and type *angela@ogcproperties.com* and press **Enter.**

    c. Observe that the IM address is added to the business card.

    d. In the **Phone numbers** section, in the **Home** text box, click and type *585–555–5555*

    e. On the **Contact** tab, in the **Options** group, click **Business Card.**

    f. If necessary, in the **Location Information** dialog box, in the **What area code (or city code) are you in now** text box, click and type *06430* and click **OK.**

    g. If necessary, in the **Phone and Modem Options** dialog box, click **OK.**

    h. In the **Edit Business Card** dialog box, in the **Fields** list box, click the **Home Phone** field.

    i. In the **Edit** section, to the right of the **Label** text box, in the drop-down list, verify that **Right** is selected.

---

2. Add the Angela.jpg image and change the background color of the business card.

    a. In the **Card Design** section, next to **Image,** click **Change.**

    b. In the **Add Card Picture** dialog box, navigate to the C:\084574Data\Managing Information at Work with Microsoft Outlook 2010 folder, select **Angela.jpg,** and click **OK.**

    c. In the **Card Design** section, from the **Image Align** drop-down list, select **Fit to Edge.**

d.   Observe that the image is inserted and is displayed on the left side of the business card.

e.   In the **Card Design** section, click the **Background Color** button.

f.   In the **Color** dialog box, in the **Basic Colors** section, select the sixth color in the last row and click **OK.**

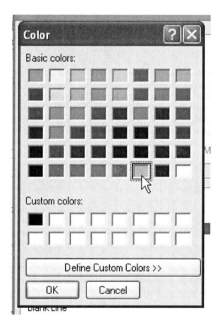

3.   Format the name and label text.

a.   In the **Fields** list box, select **Full Name,** and in the **Edit** section, click the **Italic** button to italicize the name.

b. Click the **Font Color** button, and in the **Color** dialog box, in the **Basic Colors** section, select the fifth color in the third row and click **OK.**

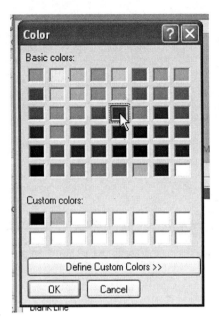

c. In the **Edit Business Card** dialog box, click **OK** to apply the formatting.

d. On the **Contact** tab, in the **Actions** group, click the **Save & Close** button.

ACTIVITY 6-6
Including a Business Card in a Personal Signature

Before You Begin:
Display the Inbox.

Scenario:
Being the director of the marketing department of a company, you need to share your contact information with clients. Therefore, you want to include your business card in your signature so that the business card is automatically included in all of the messages being sent from your Inbox.

1. Create a new signature.

   a. Select the **File** tab and choose **Options** to display the **Outlook Options** dialog box.

   b. In the **Outlook Options** dialog box, select the **Mail** tab, and in the **Compose messages** section, click **Signatures.**

   c. In the **Signatures and Stationery** dialog box, on the **E-mail Signature** tab, below the **Select signature to edit** list box, click **New.**

   d. In the **New Signature** dialog box, in the **Type a name for this signature** text box, type *Angela* and click **OK.**

   e. In the **Edit signature** text area, click and type *Regards,* and press **Enter.**

   f. Type *Angela* and press **Enter.**

2. Insert the Angela Barry business card in the signature.

   a. On the **Edit signature** toolbar, click **Business Card.**

   b. In the **Insert Business Card** dialog box, in the **Filed As** list, select **Barry, Angela** and click **OK.**

   c. In the **Edit signature** section, verify that the business card of Angela Barry is inserted below the signature text.

3. Set the option to automatically insert the signature in all the outgoing email messages.

   a. In the **Choose default signature** section, from the **New messages** drop-down list, select **Angela.**

   b. From the **Replies/forwards** drop-down list, select **Angela** and click **OK.**

   c. In the **Outlook Options** dialog box, click **OK.**

4. Check whether the business card is used with the signature.

   a. Switch to the Mail view.

   b. On the **Home** tab, in the **New** group, click **New E mail.**

c. Observe that the new message form is opened with the signature and business card of Angela Barry inserted in the message body.

d. Close the email message.

TOPIC E
Add RSS Feeds

You worked with SharePoint content from the Outlook environment. Now, you want to collect information from various websites and receive updates in your Outlook Inbox. In this topic, you will add RSS feeds through Outlook 2010.

When you are designing a project, you may have to collect and browse through information from various websites. Rather than browsing separately through each website, you can collect information through Outlook. This helps you receive information, without revealing your email address to any of the site owners.

Really Simple Syndication Feeds

Really Simple Syndication (RSS) is a method for distributing information in a standardized XML format. This XML format allows you to publish information just once so that the information can then be viewed by subscribers by using various client software programs such as Outlook. These programs are known as RSS aggregators or RSS readers, and the delivery method for RSS content is known as an *RSS feed.*

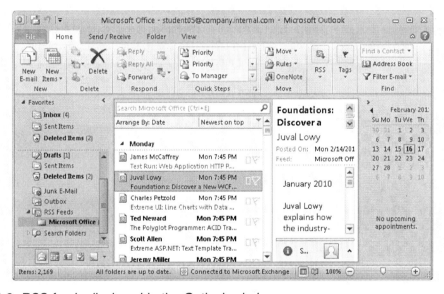

Figure 6-9: *RSS feeds displayed in the Outlook window.*

Outlook 2010 includes the functionality of an RSS aggregator. You can get RSS feeds that you subscribed to from the RSS Feeds folder in the Navigation pane. When the sites publish content, they update the RSS feed, and users who subscribed to the feed will get a list of the newly published content. You can use RSS feeds to keep up with websites, news sites, or blogs that you frequently read.

How to Add RSS Feeds

Procedure Reference: Add an RSS Feed Through Outlook 2010

To add an RSS feed through Outlook 2010:

1. Select the **File** tab and choose **Info.**
2. In the **Info** section, click **Account Settings,** and from the displayed list, select **Account Settings.**
3. In the **Account Settings** dialog box, on the **RSS Feeds** tab, click **New.**
4. In the **New RSS Feed** dialog box, in the text box, type the RSS feed link and click **Add** to display the **RSS Feed Options** dialog box.
5. In the **RSS Feed Options** dialog box, specify the settings for the RSS feed.
   - In the **General** section, in the **Feed Name** text box, type the desired name.
   - If necessary, in the **Delivery Location** section, click **Change Folder,** and in the **New RSS Feed Delivery Location** dialog box, choose a location for the RSS Feeds folder or create a new RSS Feeds folder and click **OK.**
   - In the **Downloads** section, check the **Automatically download enclosures for this RSS feed** check box to download all the articles attached to the feed.
   - Check the **Download the full article as an .html attachment** check box to download the article attached to the feed as an HTML file.
   - If necessary, in the **Update Limit** section, check the **Use the publisher update recommendation** check box for updating the feed every one hour.
6. Click **OK** to add the feed.
7. In the **Account Settings** dialog box, click **Close.**
8. If necessary, in the Navigation pane, in the **Mail Folders** section, expand the RSS Feeds folder and select the particular feed folder to view feeds.

Procedure Reference: Share an RSS Feed with Other Users

To share an RSS feed with other users:

1. In the Navigation pane, in the **Mail Folders** section, expand the RSS Feeds folder.
2. Select the desired feed folder and open the feed article that you want to share.
3. On the **RSS Article** tab of the **RSS Article** form, in the **Respond** group, click **Share This Feed.**
4. In the **RSS Feed - Share** form, in the **To** text box, type the name of the user, and if necessary enter the message text.
5. Click **Send** to share the RSS feed.

Procedure Reference: Add an RSS Feed Received from Other Users

To add an RSS feed received from other users:

1. Display the Inbox and open the message with an article attached as an RSS feed.
2. On the **RSS Article** tab of the **RSS Article** form, in the **Open** group, click **Add This Feed.**
3. If necessary, in the **Microsoft Outlook** dialog box, click **Advanced,** and in the **RSS Feed Options** dialog box, configure the options for the RSS feed.
4. In the **Microsoft Outlook** dialog box, click **Yes** to add the RSS feed to Outlook.

ACTIVITY 6-7
Adding an RSS Feed to Outlook 2010

Scenario:
Your work involves keeping yourself updated with business information. You learn that Outlook 2010 includes the functionality to of an RSS reader. You want to use this functionality to read the RSS feeds that you need.

1. Add an RSS feed to your account.

   a. Select the **File** tab and verify that **Info** is selected.

   b. In the **Info** section, click **Account Settings,** and from the drop-down list, select **Account Settings.**

   c. In the **Account Settings** dialog box, select the **RSS Feeds** tab, and on the **RSS Feeds** tab, click **New.**

   d. In the **New RSS Feed** dialog box, in the text box, type *http://msdn.microsoft.com/magazine/rss/default.aspx* and click **Add.**

   e. In the **RSS Feed Options** dialog box, in the **General** section, in the **Feed Name** text box, type *Microsoft Office*

   f. Click **OK** to add the feed and close the **RSS Feed Options** dialog box.

   g. In the **Account Settings** dialog box, click **Close.**

2. View the RSS feeds.

   a. In the Navigation pane, expand the **RSS Feeds** folder.

   b. Select the **Microsoft Office** folder to view the displayed items.

   c. Click an RSS feed to read it.

    It may take a while for the RSS feeds to appear based on your Internet speed.

   d. Close the Outlook application.

Lesson 6 Follow-up

In this lesson, you managed various tasks using the new features of Outlook. The knowledge of the new features and their functionalities will give you the confidence to use these features when you are working with the latest version of Outlook.

1. **Which Outlook tools do you expect to use the most often to manage your email messages?**

2. **Which features in Outlook do you think will help you the most in scheduling meetings?**

7 Sharing Microsoft Office 2010 Files

Lesson Time: 30 minutes

Lesson Objectives:

In this lesson, you will share files using Microsoft Office 2010.

You will:

- Protect files.
- Share files.

Introduction

You communicated information to others through email. There may be instances when you want to share files for a group to work together. Office 2010 provides features that enable you to share files safely and securely when collaborating with others. In this lesson, you will protect and share Office files.

Irrespective of what software you use to create a file, you may need to protect the file against unauthorized access and modification, and also prevent virus or malware infections. You can use the enhanced protection and sharing options packaged with Office 2010 to authenticate and share content in a secure manner.

TOPIC A
Protect Files

You shared information through email. When sharing files, it is important to ensure the safety and integrity of files and their content. In this topic, you will protect files.

When data is easily accessible to multiple users, it runs the risk of being tampered with or lost. Protecting files gives you the flexibility to share them knowing that the data is secure.

The Document Inspector

Files usually contain hidden details such as the author and company name, the comments placed, presentation notes, and other document properties, which you may not want to share with other users. The *Document Inspector* dialog box allows you to check for and remove embedded information from documents to prevent other users from viewing or retrieving such information.

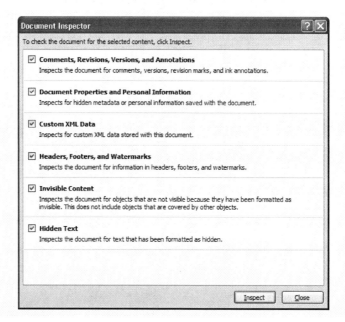

Figure 7-1: The Document Inspector dialog box.

Types of Hidden Data

Microsoft Office 2010 files can contain the following types of hidden data and personal information.

Information Type	Function of the Document Inspector
Comments and Annotations	Deletes comments and annotations.

Information Type	Function of the Document Inspector
Document Properties and Personal Information	Scans and removes file properties such as the author name, the subject and title of a file, statistical information such as the number of slides and hidden slides, and other details such as the person who last saved the file. In addition, it can find information such as the creation date and the location of the file.
Custom XML Data	Removes custom XML data that is not visible in a file. This XML data defines the structure and visual appearance of any data in the file.
Invisible On-Slide Content in Microsoft PowerPoint	Scans and removes the objects in a presentation that are formatted as invisible.
Off-Slide Content in Microsoft PowerPoint	Checks a presentation and removes the objects that are outside the slide area. These objects are not visible because of their placement. Objects may include text boxes, clip art images, graphics, and tables. However, objects to which animation effects are added are not checked.
Presentation Notes in Microsoft PowerPoint	Checks and removes any text that is present in the notes section. Presentation notes are often added as reminders for the presenter and are not necessary.

The Mark as Final Feature

The *Mark as Final* feature enables you to save a file as the final version and make it read-only. Marking a file as final ensures that the file is not tampered with when it is shared. When you open a file that is marked final, an alert message appears below the ribbon tabs with an **Edit Anyway** button. You can click this button to make modifications to the file.

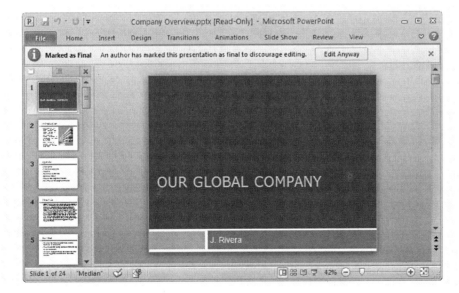

Figure 7-2: A presentation marked as final.

Information Rights Management

Information Rights Management (IRM) is a feature that helps you prevent sensitive information from being manipulated by unauthorized recipients. You can restrict permission to access a file using this feature. IRM also provides options to prohibit printing, forwarding, or copying of sensitive data, and even capturing screens using the Print Screen feature of Windows. You can also set an expiration date to restrict file access after a specific time. These restrictions are carried along with the presentation or document as part of the file. All data present in a file is bound by these permissions.

Digital Signatures

A *digital signature* is a digital stamp that authenticates the identity of a file's sender to ensure the integrity of the file. It indicates that the content of the file is unchanged since the file was stamped with the signature. You can add either a visible or an invisible digital signature to a presentation. In PowerPoint, the signature icon on the status bar indicates that the presentation is digitally signed. When you open a digitally signed presentation, the details of the digital signature are displayed in the **Signatures** pane. You cannot make modifications to the presentation until the digital signature is removed.

How to Protect Files

Procedure Reference: Inspect a File

To inspect a file:

1. Ensure that the file that needs to be inspected is saved.
2. Select the **File** tab and choose **Info.**
3. In the Information pane, from the **Check for Issues** drop-down list, select **Inspect Document.**
4. In the **Document Inspector** dialog box, check or uncheck the desired check boxes to check for specific type of information and click **Inspect.**
5. In the **Review the inspection results** section, click **Remove All** to remove information such as comments and annotations, document properties and personal information, and metadata information.
6. If necessary, click **Reinspect** and repeat steps 4 through 6 to reinspect the presentation.
7. Click **Close.**

Procedure Reference: Mark a Presentation as Final

To mark a presentation as final:

1. Select the **File** tab and choose **Info.**
2. In the Information pane, from the **Protect Presentation** drop-down list, select **Mark as Final.**
3. In the **Microsoft PowerPoint** message box, click **OK** to mark the presentation as final and observe that the file changes to the Read-only mode.

ACTIVITY 7-1

Restricting Document Access

Data Files:

C:\084574Data\Sharing Microsoft Office 2010 Files\OGC Information.pptx

Scenario:

Your manager has given his feedback on the presentation that you are working on. Now, you want the other functional managers to give their feedback too, but you do not want them to view your manager's comments. Therefore, before sending the presentation to the other managers, you decide to remove all the comments and personal information from it.

---

1. Inspect the presentation.

   a. Launch the PowerPoint application.

   b. Navigate to the C:\084574Data\Sharing Microsoft Office 2010 Files folder and open the OGC Information.pptx file.

   c. Select the **File** tab.

   d. Observe that the author information is displayed in the Backstage view, and in the Information pane, from the **Check for Issues** drop-down list, select **Inspect Document.**

   e. In the **Document Inspector** dialog box, uncheck the **Custom XML Data** check box to avoid checking for XML data.

   f. Check the **Off-Slide Content** check box to inspect for objects that are outside the slide area.

   g. Click **Inspect** to inspect the presentation.

h.   Observe that the slide contains comments, document properties, personal information, and presentation notes.

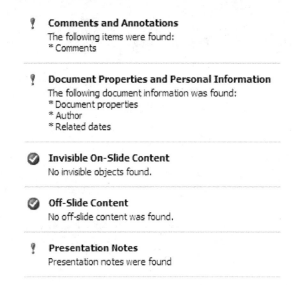

2.   Remove document information and reinspect the presentation.

a.   In the **Comments and Annotations** section, click **Remove All.**

b.   In the **Document Properties and Personal Information** section, click **Remove All.**

c.   In the **Presentation Notes** section, click **Remove All.**

d.   Click **Reinspect** and then click **Inspect** to confirm the changes.

e.   In the **Document Inspector** dialog box, observe that all hidden data and personal information is removed and click **Close.**

f.   Observe that the author information displayed in the Backstage view is removed.

g.   On the **File** tab, click **Save As.**

h.   In the **Save As** dialog box, in the **File name** text box, type *My OGC Information.pptx* and click **Save.**

3.   Mark the presentation as final.

a.   Select the **File** tab, in the Information pane, from the **Protect Presentation** drop-down list, select **Mark as Final.**

b.   In the **Microsoft PowerPoint** message box, click **OK** to confirm that the presentation can be marked as final.

c.   In the **Microsoft PowerPoint** message box, click **OK.**

d.   Observe that the Backstage view displays a message stating that the presentation is marked as final.

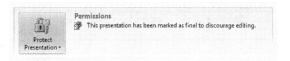

e. Select the **Home** tab, and on the status bar, observe that an icon is displayed,  indicating that the presentation is marked final.

Marked as Final   An author has marked this presentation as final to discourage editing.   Edit Anyway

f. Observe the message indicating that the file cannot be edited because it is marked as final, and close the presentation.

TOPIC B
Share Files

You protected files to ensure authority over them. You may need the flexibility to share, open, and edit documents from any location, even without the access to the Office application. In this topic, you will share files using Office Web Apps.

Imagine you create a document and want to implement the changes suggested by your colleagues. Normally, it is a lengthy process to send files, get feedback, and incorporate the feedback. Wouldn't it be nice if you and your colleagues could work in the same document simultaneously? Saving your files to the web using Office Web Apps not only ensures that anyone can access them, but also allows everyone to work with the files in real time.

The Save to SkyDrive Feature

Microsoft Office 2010 allows you to save files to the web using a Windows Live ID. You can sign in to SkyDrive by entering your Windows Live credentials to access the saved file from any other computer and from any location. You can view or edit using Office Web Apps, or download files to edit them using the Office 2010 application.

Co-authoring

In Office 2010, co-authoring is a new feature that allows multiple people to view and edit a file at the same time. Both Word and PowerPoint support this feature. To use this feature, the file should be saved either on Windows Live SkyDrive or SharePoint 2010.

Windows Live SkyDrive

Windows Live SkyDrive is an online repository that lets you save files and share them with other users. To access SkyDrive, you need to have a Windows Live ID.

Office Mobile 2010

Office Mobile 2010 is a feature that allows you to work on Office files using an enhanced mobile version of the Word, Excel, or PowerPoint application. With Office Mobile 2010, you can easily open, view, edit, and copy and paste information in a file. You can also email Office documents from your mobile device or post them to your SharePoint workspace. Office Mobile 2010 is not part of Office 2010, but the application will be available with the release of Office 2010 for phones using Windows Mobile 6.5 or later.

How to Share Files

Procedure Reference: Save a File to Windows Live SkyDrive

To save a file to Windows Live SkyDrive:

1. Select the **File** tab and choose **Save & Send.**

2. In the Backstage view, in the left pane, select the **Save to Web** option.

3. In the right pane, click **Sign In** and enter your Windows Live credentials.

4. In the **My Folders** section, select the folder in which you want to save the file and click **Save As.**

5. In the **Save As** dialog box, type the name of the file and click **Save.**

Procedure Reference: Access and Work with Office Files on the Web

To access and work with Office files on the web:

1. Open the web browser of your choice.

2. In the Address bar, type the address as *http://skydrive.live.com.*

3. Enter your Windows Live credentials.

4. Browse to the location where the file is saved, select the file that you want to view, and click **View.**

5. At the bottom of the Internet Explorer window, click the **Open in browser** button to make changes to the file.

6. After making the necessary edits, at the right corner of the browser window, click the sign out link to log out of Windows Live SkyDrive.

ACTIVITY 7-2
Saving Presentations to the Web

Data Files:

C:\084574Data\Sharing Microsoft Office 2010 Files\OGC Properties Overview.pptx

Scenario:

You have completed work on a presentation. You plan to send the presentation through email to a reviewer in a different location. However, you are aware that the reviewer does not have the Office 2010 suite installed. You decide to share the presentation on the web so that he can access it without having to install the Office 2010 suite.

---

1. Log in to Windows Live SkyDrive.

   a. Navigate to the C:\084574Data\Sharing Microsoft Office 2010 Files folder and open the OGC Properties Overview.pptx file.

   b. Select the **File** tab and choose **Save & Send.**

   c. In the **Save & Send** pane, select the **Save to Web** option.

   d. In the **Save to Windows Live** pane, click **Sign In.**

   e. In the **Connecting to docs.live.net** dialog box, in the **E-mail address** text box, type your Windows Live ID, and in the **Password** text box, type your password and click **OK.**

---

2. Save the file to SkyDrive.

   a. In the **Save to Windows Live SkyDrive** pane, in the **Shared Folders** section, select the **Public** folder and click **Save As.**

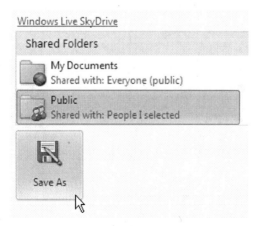

   b. In the **Save As** dialog box, in the **Save in** text box, observe that the SkyDrive location where the file will be saved is displayed.

   c. Save the file as *OGC File for Review.pptx* and close it.

---

d. Save the file as ***OGC File for Review.pptx***, close it, and then close the PowerPoint application.

ACTIVITY 7-3
Working with Shared Presentations on the Web

Scenario:
You have saved a presentation on the web. Before you send information about the presentation and its location to the reviewer, you want to preview the presentation on the web to ensure that all the necessary details are entered. Therefore, you decide to access the presentation from the Internet.

---

1. Display the OGC for Review.pptx presentation from a web browser.

    a. Choose **Start→Internet.**

    b. In the Internet Explorer window, in the Address bar, type ***http://skydrive.live.com*** and press **Enter.**

    c. On the **Windows Live** page, at the top-right corner, click **Sign in.**

    d. On the **Welcome to Windows Live** page, in the **sign in** section, in the **Windows Live ID** text box, type your user name and press **Tab.**

    e. In the **Password** text box, type your password and click **Sign in.**

    f. In the **My Files — Windows Live** page, select the **Public** folder to view the file.

---

2. View and edit the presentation.

    a. Select the **OGC File for Review** file to view it.

    b. Close the **Improve Your Experience** message bar.

    c. At the bottom of the Internet Explorer window, click the **Next Slide** button to navigate to the next slide.

    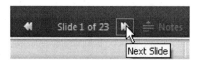

    d. Click **Edit in Browser** to edit the presentation in the Internet Explorer window.

    e. On the displayed slide, select the bulleted list.

    f. On the **Home** tab, in the **Font** group, click the **Italic** button.

g. In the **Font** group, from the **Font color** gallery, in the **Theme Colors** section, select the **ba8e2c** color, which is the sixth color in the fifth row, and click away from the bulleted list to view the change.

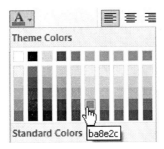

h. Select the **File** tab and choose **Close** to close the presentation.

i. Sign out of your Windows Live account and close the browser window.

Lesson 7 Follow-up

In this lesson, you saved a document to the web and viewed it by using Office Web Apps. Office Web Apps provides you with the flexibility to authenticate, access, share, and modify Office files on the fly and also allows multiple users to work on files simultaneously.

1. **How do you think the Save to SkyDrive feature is beneficial to you?**

2. **What are the advantages of securing a file before sharing?**

Follow-up

In this course, you customized the redesigned user interface and modified documents using the Microsoft Word application. You also added visual elements to the slides in a PowerPoint presentation. Additionally, you saved Office application files to the web so that they can be accessed by users who do not have Microsoft Office installed on their workstations. These skills will enable you to use various user friendly features available in Microsoft Office 2010 and will help work with various Office applications.

1. **How do the new features of Office 2010 help reduce the time taken to carry out various functions?**

2. **Where might you become more efficient while working in a document by using the new features in PowerPoint 2010?**

3. **How will you use the new features in Access 2010 for developing databases in your organization?**

What's Next?

This course does not form part of any specific series.

Lesson Labs

Lesson labs are provided as an additional learning resource for this course. The labs may or may not be performed as part of the classroom activities. Your instructor will consider setup issues, classroom timing issues, and instructional needs to determine which labs are appropriate for you to perform, and at what point during the class. If you do not perform the labs in class, your instructor can tell you if you can perform them independently as self-study, and if there are any special setup requirements.

Lesson 1 Lab 1

Getting Started with the Microsoft Office 2010 Application Interface

Activity Time: 15 minutes

Data Files:

C:\084574Data\Getting Started with Microsoft Office 2010\OGC Properties.docx, enus_084574_01_1_solution.zip

Scenario:

You are working on the Book.docx file in the Word application. To simplify the functionality, you want to add certain commands to the Quick Access toolbar. You decide to format the appearance of the title by previewing the various options in the gallery. After printing a copy of the document, you want to save a new copy of the original document in earlier Word format just to make sure that you can work with it in other workstations that may not have Word 2010 installed.

1. Open the Book.docx file from the C:\084574Data\Getting Started with Microsoft Office 2010 folder.

2. Add the **New** command to the Quick Access toolbar.

3. Apply bold formatting to the word "OGC" in the second paragraph, using the Mini toolbar.

4. Apply the **Heading 1** Quick style to the title text "Get Published."

5. Preview the document in portrait orientation and print it.

6. Save the document as *My Book.doc* in the **Word 97–2003 Document (*.doc)** format.

Lesson 2 Lab 1

Working with Documents Using Microsoft Word 2010

Activity Time: 10 minutes

Data Files:

C:\084574Data\Modifying Documents\OGC Annual Report.docx, enus_084574_02_1_ datafile.zip

Scenario:

You are working on the OGC Annual Report.docx document. You want to add style enhancements to the text for better visual appeal. Also, you want to add a SmartArt graphic for better illustration and make changes to the structure of the document using the **Navigation** pane.

---

1. Open the *OGC Annual Report.docx* file from the C:\084574Data\Modifying Documents folder.

---

2. Use the **Navigation** pane to promote the title "Market Forecast," which is present on the third page.

---

3. Insert a SmartArt **Linear Venn** under the heading "Strategy," above the caption "Figure A," and enter the text *Residential, Rental, Corporate,* and *Relocation* in the shapes.

---

4. Create a quick style named *ogc_prop* and apply it to the title "OGC Properties, Inc" and add it to the **Styles** gallery.

---

5. Save the file as *My OGC Annual Report.docx* and close it.

Lesson 3 Lab 1
Presenting Data in a Spreadsheet

Activity Time: 10 minutes

Data Files:

C:\084574\Data\Working with Spreadsheets\Revenue Summary.xlsx, C:\084574\Data\Working with Spreadsheets\Revenue.xlsx, enus_084574_03_1_datafiles.zip

Scenario:

You need to analyze and prepare a report on the previous year's revenue summary of your company. Before making decisions based on figures, you decide to highlight and classify the low, medium, and high revenue figures and also filter the highest revenue figures from the data. Additionally, you need to calculate the average high revenue figure for the first quarter.

---

1. Open the Revenue Summary.xlsx file from the C:\084574\Data\Working with Spreadsheetsfolder.

---

2. Convert the entire range of data to a table.

---

3. Apply appropriate icon sets to conditionally format the sales figures.

---

4. Sort data by the color of the icon to analyze data.

---

5. Filter the revenue values for January and February.

---

6. Save the Excel workbook as **My Revenue Summary.xlsx** and close it.

---

7. Open the Revenue.xlsx file from the C:\084574\Data\Working with Spreadsheetsfolder.

---

8. In the Revenue.xlsx workbook, in the European Sales worksheet, create a column chart for the data.

---

9. In the Revenue.xlsx workbook, in the European Sales worksheet, insert a Line Sparkline to display the sales trend for each region.

---

10. Add a high point for the Sparkline and format the Sparkline by applying a chart style.

---

11. Create a PivotTable and PivotChart based on the Revenue worksheet to analyze sales data by month and sales.

---

12. Save the Excel workbook as *My Revenue.xlsx* and close it.

Lesson 4 Lab 1
Creating Dynamic Presentations

Activity Time: 10 minutes

Data Files:

C:\084574Data\Creating Dynamic Presentations\Information.pptx, enus_084574_04_1_datafiles.zip

Scenario:

While reviewing a presentation, you find that it is not in the correct format and is not visually appealing. You want to change the layout to suit the overall theme of the presentation. You also want to apply some graphical effects to enhance the visual appearance of the presentation.

1. Open the Information.pptx file from the C:\084574Data\Creating Dynamic Presentations folder.

2. Apply the Civic theme to the presentation.

3. Create and apply a custom theme color with the following specifications and save the custom theme as *Company Theme Color.*
   - Text/Background - Dark 2: Olive Green, Accent 3
   - Accent 1: Tan, Text 2, Darker 50%
   - Accent 2: Dark Blue, Background 2, Lighter 60%

4. Apply the **Inside Diagonal Bottom Right** shadow effect in slide 8.

5. Save the presentation as *My Information.ppsx* and close it.

Lesson 5 Lab 1
Working with Databases

Activity Time: 10 minutes

Data Files:

C:\084574Data\Working with Databases\Inventory.accdb, enus_084574_05_1_datafiles.zip

Scenario:

You want to examine the procurement price for the inventory in your organization and generate a report that can be used as a quick reference when needed. You also want to export the data to a text file so that you can share the inventory data with others who do not have Microsoft Access 2010.

1. Open the Inventory.accdb file from the C:\084574Data\Working with Databases folder.

2. Create a report with fields for the manufacturer ID, manufacturer name, current years' purchase price, and previous years' purchase price.

3. Group the data by manufacturer.

4. Apply a custom border to the fields that appear in the detail section of the Computers report.

5. Apply conditional formatting to the report using data bars for the purchase prices for the current and previous years.

6. Export the data in a text format and save the text file as *Inventory Data.txt* in the text format.

7. Save and close the database.

Lesson 6 Lab 1

Managing Your Calendar in Outlook

Activity Time: 10 minutes

Scenario:

Being the HR manager, you need to attend a meeting scheduled in your head office regarding HR policies. Because you will be out of the office for a week, you want to give the Reviewer access to your personal assistant to enable her to manage and maintain your schedule. Also, you are to interview a candidate for the Multimedia Developer position. You decide to schedule a meeting for the same, and because there are other managers who will also be on the interviewing panel for the candidate, you decide to share your calendar with them so that they can view your schedule in case there are any changes to be made to the schedule.

1. Schedule a meeting with the required and optional attendees with the subject "Interview for the Multimedia Developer position." for an hour in a conference room.

2. Share your calendar with two other users.

3. Delegate access to your calendar to a user.

4. Set the Reviewer permission to the delegate for accessing your calendar.

Lesson 7 Lab 1

Sharing Presentations Through the Web

Activity Time: 10 minutes

Data Files:

C:\084574Data\Sharing Microsoft Office 2010 Files\OGC Overview.pptx, enus_084574_06_1_datafiles.zip, enus_084574_06_1_solution.zip

Before You Begin:

To perform this activity, you must have a registered Windows Live ID and an Internet connection.

Scenario:

Now that the presentation is complete, you need to send it for review. You need feedback for this presentation by next week, but your reviewer is out of the office. You decide to save the presentation on the web for your reviewer to access and preview the presentation online.

---

1. Open the OGC Overview.pptx file from the C:\084574Data\Sharing Microsoft Office 2010 Files folder.

---

2. Mark the presentation as final.

---

3. Save the file to the Public folder in your SkyDrive account.

---

4. Open a web browser and access the SkyDrive account using **http://skydrive.live.com**.

---

5. Navigate to the file available in the Public folder.

---

6. View the file from SkyDrive.

Glossary

alternate background color

A feature using which you can set a specific color for every other row in a table.

anchoring

A feature that enables you to tie a control or a section of a control to another control so that you can move and resize them simultaneously.

Animation Painter

A command that allows you to replicate the animation of the existing objects on a slide on other objects.

Animation Pane

A pane that provides options to add an animation effect, and remove, change, or even reorder an animation effect that is applied.

Application Parts

A gallery that lists database objects such as tables, queries, reports, and forms as templates.

Attachment data type

A new data type that enables you to store external documents and binary files in a record, and attach multiple files to a single record.

Auto Calendar

An icon that appears at the right side of the Date/Time data type field when you select the field and displays a calendar when you click it.

Backstage view

An interface that contains a series of tabs that group similar commands, displays the compatibility, permissions, and version information of a file, and contains options to save, share, print, and publish files.

calendar group

An option in the Calendar view that allows you to view multiple calendars of other users together so as to compare their schedules before you schedule a meeting.

calendar overlays

An option of viewing multiple calendars at the same time.

client objects

The objects that do not refer to any web objects and all the elements of a client object are not visible as a web object.

Compare

A feature that is used to combine or compare different versions of a document and to check for information that might have been deleted, modified, moved, or replaced in the original document.

Compatibility Checker

A feature that allows you to identify the compatibility of objects and data that are saved in an earlier version of Office.

conditional formatting
The formatting applied to cells dynamically by Excel 2010 based on conditions that the data in the cells fulfill.

contextual tabs
The tabs with specialized commands that are displayed when the object they operate on is selected.

Conversation
A view that enables you to view groups of messages that share the same subject.

data macro
A feature that allows you to attach macros to table data.

data type
A categorization of data associated with a particular field based on certain predefined characteristics.

Data Type
A gallery that displays common field types such as attachment and currency, and used for inserting a new field into a table.

dialog box launchers
The small buttons that help you launch the relevant dialog boxes with advanced setting options.

digital signature
A digital stamp that indicates that the contents of a file are not modified.

Document Inspector
A dialog box that enables you to scan and remove personal information, comments, hidden data, and tracked changes within a file.

EBC
(Electronic Business Card) The electronic version of the business card that displays contact details.

embedded macros
The macros that are part of the property attached to an event.

Expression Builder
A dialog box that allows you to select database objects and build formulas and calculations that are used with queries and reports.

Field Insertion
A feature with which you can easily insert a new field by typing the field name in the first row of a new column in the Datasheet view.

filter
A feature that enables you to filter data based on the data type in a column.

Formula AutoComplete
A dynamic feature that allows you to conveniently choose and enter formulas and functions.

Formula Bar
An interface component of Excel 2010 that contains the Name Box and the Insert Function button, and is used for specifying formulas.

gallery
A library that lists elements of the same category.

Instant Search
A feature that allows you to quickly search for items in Outlook by specifying certain search criteria.

IntelliSense
A feature in Access 2010 that allows you to build expressions by automatically displaying the expression that you might use in a given context when you type.

IRM
(Information Rights Management) A feature in Microsoft Office applications that allows users to have control over sensitive information in their Office files.

ligatures
The two letter characters that are formed into one by joining the letters.

Live Preview

A feature that enables you to view the results of editing and formatting changes made to an Office application, without actually applying them.

Macro Designer

A macro builder tool that enables you to create macros easily.

macros

The instructions that result in a series of instructions in machine language.

Mark as Final

A feature that enables you to save a file as the final and latest version and also convert the file to read-only mode.

Mini toolbar

A floating toolbar that is displayed beside selected text, and consists of commonly used font and paragraph formatting tools.

modules

The self contained components that are used in combination with other components.

navigation form

A layout that allows you to navigate within objects in an application.

options for importing data

The options located in the Import & Link group on the External Data tab that enable you to import data from various data sources into Access.

PivotChart

A chart whose data can be reoriented, analyzed, and dynamically represented.

PivotTable

A table whose fields can be reoriented for performing selective analysis.

Property Sheet Pane

A collection of tools that enables you to set properties for the controls in a form such as a text box, image, label, or combo box.

Quick Access

A toolbar that provides easy access to core commands such as Save, Undo, and Repeat.

quick step

A command that facilitates performing common tasks that involve multiple actions as a single-click option.

Quick Styles

A command that contains sets of styles packaged together to apply a set of design and formatting changes to text.

Report

A command that allows you to create reports using data from various query results.

Ribbon

A panel at the top portion of a document that contains a selection of easy-to-browse commands, which you may need to work on a document.

rich text memo property

A property that enables better formatting of data in tables that are stored in memo fields.

RSS feed

A delivery method for RSS content.

RSS

(Really Simple Syndication) A method for distributing information in a standardized XML format.

Schedule

A calendar view that allows you to view multiple calendars to compare schedules.

Screenshot

A tool that allows you to capture an image of any window on a computer and insert it into a document.

ScreenTip

A description of the task performed by the tool when the mouse pointer is placed over the tool.

Send a Calendar via E-mail

A dialog box that allows you to send calendars to other users in an email message.

Slicers

A feature that enables you to slice data and include only the elements you want in Pivot-Tables and PivotCharts.

Slide Section

A slide section is a collection of similar types of slides in a presentation which are used to organize a presentation.

SmartArt graphics

The layouts that are used to show a time line or developmental progression, or the sequential steps in a process or workflow.

Sparklines

The miniature charts that appear within the worksheet, depicting the numbers in a worksheet table.

Sparklines

The type of information graphics that can be characterized by their small size and high data density. They are tiny, word-sized charts that can appear in a cell.

stacked layouts

The form layouts that display controls vertically.

status bar

A frame that displays a number of options and information relating to document functionality in a well-organized manner.

stylistic sets

The styles that can be applied to a font to give it a slightly different look in a document.

tabular layouts

The form layouts that display controls in a horizontal table format with one row per record.

Themes

A command that contains themes packaged together to apply a set of colors, fonts, and effects to a document.

themes

The design templates that provide a consistent visual look and feel for a presentation.

To-Do Bar

A bar that displays the calendar, upcoming appointments, and a list of tasks.

Totals

A feature that enables you to add a Totals row to a report.

transitions

The special effects that appear while navigating through a slide show.

Tri-Pane Review

A panel that is used to view and compare two different versions of a document along with the view that combines the changes from each of the two compared documents.

VBA

(Visual Basic for Applications) An implementation of various event-driven programming languages such as Visual Basic 6 and logical connection with the integrated development environment (IDE).

Video Tools

A group of commands used to edit, modify and format videos.

Web Browser Control

A control tool that allows you to view web content within the Access 2010 application.

Web Compatibility Checker

A feature that enables you to identify whether the web database objects that you create are supported on the web.

web objects

The database objects such as a form, table, query, or report in a web database.

WordArt

The effects applied to text in a Word document to increase the visual appeal of text in the document.

WYSIWYG

(What You See Is What You Get) A feature that enables you to modify the layouts in a form when you are working on it.

XML

A robust file format that allows you to easily integrate it with other applications.

Index

A

animation effects, 116
  applying, 118
  changing, 118
Animation Painter
  animating objects, 118
Application Parts, 153
  building a database, 154
Attachment data type, 135
Auto Calendar, 135

B

Backstage view
  print options, 27

C

calendar groups, 198
calendar overlays, 198
chart enhancements, 83
chart templates, 85
chart tools, 84
charts
  creating, 85
client objects, 172
commands
  Animation Painter, 116
  Clean Up, 184
  Ignore, 184
  Quick Styles, 39
  Report, 158
  Themes, 40
conditional formatting, 79
  applying, 80
contextual tab groups, 15
contextual tabs, 14

formatting an object, 18

D

data macros, 144
Data Type, 135
data types, 135
databases
  creating a multivalued field, 138
  creating a table, 137
delegates, 198
dialog box launchers, 4
dialog boxes
  Advanced Find, 192
  Document Inspector, 222
  Edit Business Card, 208
  Expression Builder, 145
  Send a Calendar via E-mail, 197

E

EBC, 207
embedded macros, 144
Excel table enhancements, 68
export options, 167
  exporting data to a text file, 169

F

features
  alternate background color, 136
  anchoring, 152
  Compare, 61
  Compatibility Checker, 23
  Field Insertion, 134
  Formula AutoComplete, 73
  Instant Search, 191
  IntelliSense, 145

Live Preview, 17
Mark as Final, 223
Slicers, 94
Slide Section, 127
Totals, 159
Web Compatibility Checker, 173
filters, 158
 filtering data, 161
form creation tools, 151
Formula Bar, 72
 applying a formula, 74
formula dependence, 73
formula precedence, 73

G

galleries, 16

I

IRM, 224

L

layouts
 designing a form, 154
ligatures, 42

M

Macro Designer, 144
macros, 143
 creating and running, 146
markers, 91
modules, 143

N

navigation forms, 173
 adding, 175
new text effects, 40

O

Office files
 previewing and printing, 28
options for importing data, 166
Outlook
 searching for items, 192

P

panes
 Animation Pane, 117
 Navigation, 34
paste preview options, 18

photo albums
 creating, 111
pictures
 modifying, 110
PivotCharts, 94
 creating, 96
PivotTables, 93
 creating, 95
 customizing calculations, 95
Property Sheet, 152

Q

queries
 creating, 146
quick steps, 182
 creating, 186
Quick styles
 creating, 43

R

reports
 applying conditional formatting, 161
 generating, 160
 grouping and sorting data, 160
Ribbon, 2
rich text memo property, 134
RSS, 217
RSS feeds, 217
 adding, 218
 sharing, 218

S

screenshots
 capturing, 58
ScreenTips, 6
Slicers
 inserting, 96
SmartArt graphics, 49
 applying graphic and 3D effects, 50
 inserting, 50
Sparklines, 16, 90
 creating, 91
stacked layouts, 152
status bar, 2
 customizing, 10
stylistic sets, 42

T

tabular layouts, 152
text effects
  applying, 44
themes, 104
  applying, 43
  creating a custom theme color and font, 105
  formatting, 106
To Do Bar
  displaying and customizing, 201
To-Do Bar, 196
toolbars
  customizing the Quick Access toolbar, 9
  formatting text using the Mini toolbar, 10
  Mini, 7
  Quick Access, 2
tools
  Remove Background, 57
  Screenshot, 56
  Web Browser Control, 174
transitions, 117
  applying, 118
Tri-Pane Review, 61

types of queries, 143

V

VBA, 143
video styles and effects, 123
Video Tools, 122
videos
  inserting, 123
views
  Backstage, 5
  Conversation, 183
  Schedule, 196

W

web objects, 172
WordArt, 41
  applying, 44
worksheets
  importing data, 168
WYSIWYG, 152

X

XML, 21